Your Wedding and Beyond

Ideas to Make Your Heart Sing

Natasha Hood

A Resource and Guide for Creating Meaningful Wedding

Ceremonies and Living an Inspired Marriage

FIRST EDITION

Book design by Publishing Push
Back cover photograph by Wendy Ball

ISBN: 978-1-80227-400-4 (paperback)
ISBN: 978-1-80227-401-1 (hardback)
ISBN: 978-1-80227-425-7 (eBook)

www.natashahood.com

Contents

Part Three: Post-Wedding Marriage Care and Maintenance

Introducing Natasha

It has been my long-held dream to write this book. On completing my Interfaith Minister training in 2004, I began my vocation as a celebrant. I did not even know that word when I began my training, for it was not in common parlance. What I had known was a sudden and urgent longing to co-create meaningful ceremonies and rituals with people.

It has been a rich journey ever since. I have loved co-creating bespoke wedding ceremonies with and for many couples. This work has deepened my fascination for folklore, rites of passage, and different cultures and worldviews. It has highlighted how we have lost so much connection with ritual, community, and ways of communing with spirit.

On a personal level, I have watched myself change from a young woman who resolutely believed there was no difference between the sexes beyond cultural conditioning, to one who now celebrates the differences between masculine and feminine. I once considered the institution of marriage obsolete, but now passionately reclaim the potential beauty and power of one of the most universally acknowledged life rites.

I originally envisioned this book primarily as a resource, collating customs to inspire both couples and celebrants in creating personally meaningful wedding ceremonies. However, as I have grown, so too has the scope of this book. My understanding and vision have expanded through my own journey of personal relationships and 'discovering' whole new worlds around conscious relating, healing, trauma, communication, sacred sexuality and intimacy.

I eventually realised that I am particularly interested in *the marriage that follows* the wedding. I am interested in the relationships of real people, with our struggles, joys and hopes, our blocks to love and the willingness to heal, grow and keep loving *despite* them... *This* is what inspires me - embracing our messy, hurting, kind, unskillful, doing-our-best selves and bringing ALL of it to the altar of love.

This book has evolved into both a resource for creating a transformative wedding rite as well as a guide for living married, everyday life as inspiringly and lovingly as possible.

It is an invitation to serve life and love through marriage.

Introducing This Book

This book is about both weddings and marriage. It weaves together many threads of inspiration from diverse times and cultures.

It is written for all those interested in consciously engaging with the *process* of *getting married.* It is a profound invitation to discover and <u>stand behind</u> what is personally important. *Once married*, it gives deep meaning to the inner sanctum of marriage.

A wedding is a rite of passage marking the stepping into marriage and the beginning of a new life. Marriage is the actual everyday living of shared, intimate relationship.

Marriage represents the strongest affirmation I know to express and support the deepest bond between two people. It is sacred to me, holy. A relationship has to be worthy of marriage.

The rite of marriage has been marked since time immemorial. Grievously, it has not always served love or happiness. This book, however, is offered as a joyous re-framing of one of the major life rites.

We have become impoverished in the realms of celebration, community, and ritual. By drawing on a wealth of folklore and customs, I seek to honour the gifts available to us through exploring the potential mystery, beauty and power of marriage.

My hope is that couples be empowered to create the wedding ceremony that brings their hearts and souls alive while establishing the template of the marriage to follow.

This book is dedicated to all those who hand over their partnership and marriage to love. To all those who invite spirit, life, to guide their words and actions, that we may be our greatest selves, knowing our love counts.

It is to all of us, no matter how often we have broken our vows. As Rumi[1] says: 'Come, come whoever you are, even though you've broken your vows a thousand times, come, come again.'

Welcome back! May we each answer the call to be the love that we are. May we express it through words, actions, the sanctity of our bodies, and the vows of commitment we make to the beloved companion at our side.

The Views and Thoughts in this Book

I do not espouse any particular way of thinking. I do, however, delight in sharing reflections and ideas (both my own and others) which have inspired and nourished me and which, I believe, support a culture of love and empowerment.

My focus is primarily the Western narrative, simply because it is the one I have the most access to. Furthermore, the material is not definitive, for the scope is enormous and my knowledge limited.

A Note on Sexual Orientation and Gender

This book has a heterosexual bias, as I have written from my own experience. In addition, the cultural norms described here assume marriage between a couple in the traditional roles of bride/groom and husband/wife.

---

[1] *Jalaladin Rumi – thirteenth-century Persian poet and mystic*

However, I hope it may serve any relationship or marriage with love at its core, regardless of the sexual orientation, gender, or the number of people involved. You are invited to use whatever inspires you, adapting as necessary to make it your own.

A Note on Language

It can be difficult to write about the intangible mysteries of life with language that, for many, has become outdated or even alienating. It is the challenge of expressing new-paradigm thoughts with old-paradigm language.

We are in that fertile 'betwixt-and-between' place where cultural shifts are happening rapidly, and we can all be part of co-creating that new paradigm.

The cultural wounding around words such as 'marriage,' 'husband,' 'wife,' 'bride,' 'groom,' and many others can be immense for some. They may need tender 'unpacking' in order to find healing or to reclaim them. I hope that some of the sharings in this book are a balm for those that welcome it. I also recognise this is not the path of everyone.

'God' is often another such stumbling block. I use it as being synonymous with love, or anything which inspires a sense of goodness, mystery, or 'something greater' than ourselves.

PART ONE

Reflections and Inspirations on
Weddings and Marriage

CHAPTER ONE

Why Marry?
What Weddings and Marriage Can be About

Social norms no longer require marriage. Many couples live long-term, loving and committed relationships without it. Although this book centres around marriage formally entered via the wedding rite, it also feels important to acknowledge the truth and validity of these relationships at the outset.

In his book honouring Native American traditions, Horn[2] addresses this beautifully, saying: 'No matter how two people choose to become companions, no traditional way requires a legal document that declares their marriage. None demands a state witness. None needs a mediator to stand between two people in love and the Great Holy Mystery. When the dreams and life events of two lovers intertwine, and when the feelings are right, the sacred union forms and takes place within the sacred Circle of Life.'

---

[2] *Gabriel Horn - 'The Book of Ceremonies; a Native Way of Honoring and Living the Sacred' (2005)*

Yet many couples do still choose to walk the path of formal marriage. Why, despite the absence of stigma and social pressure, might this be so? Why is marriage such an intimately cherished dream, long-held vision, even soul-calling, for some? Others consider it a vocation, even a 'ministry', recognising it as work in the service of love.

A New Paradigm

Many years ago, I was delighted to come across the concept of 'Spiritual Partnership'[3] as an alternative archetype to that of 'Marriage.' While oppression and misery are entangled within marriage's long history, spiritual partnership points to a new paradigm of equality, purpose and joy.

The concept of 'spiritual partnership' opened a door in me. Over the years, I came to realise that I am interested in the Marriage that *is* a Spiritual Partnership - one that is alive, conscious and vibrantly attuned to serving love.

It feels painful to have the two as separate, almost opposing, archetypes. What if the two were united as one? A gift of our times is the invitation to fashion whatever uniquely supports a personally meaningful version of wedding and marriage.

To me, the Spiritual Partnership-Marriage is one that recognises CONSCIOUS INTENTIONAL RELATIONSHIP AS A VEHICLE FOR HEALING AND TRANSFORMATION.

---

[3] *I believe the term 'Spiritual Partnership' was coined by Gary Zukav, American spiritual teacher and author of best-sellers including 'The Seat of the Soul' and 'Spiritual Partnership: the Journey to Authentic Power'*

The Wedding Rite

Ritual is powerful; it *does* something. It brings focus and consciousness to an act and invites surrender to something greater than ourselves. Ceremony magnifies life. Dramatically or subtly, things are never quite the same again for someone who has walked a rite of passage with an engaged heart and spirit. Entering marriage through ritual is a transformational experience.

A 'wedding' involves much more than the formal ceremony, followed by celebrations. For me, the <u>whole</u> process 'of getting married' constitutes the wedding or marriage rite. The wedding day(s) is a focal point within a much larger context and time frame of preparation and integration.

Along the way, inner and outer demands will arise, with practicalities to arrange and personal or spiritual matters to tend. To fully receive the gifts of any rite of passage, it serves well to give fulsome time and attention to all that may get touched, even 'triggered,' within us.

While this primarily applies to the couple, the shift in the relationship that is marked by a wedding affects everyone within their family and friendship circles. Assimilating the news that someone we know is getting married invariably requires some adjustment. To greater or lesser extents then, we are *all* initiates at a wedding.

This 'private' face of weddings - both for the couple <u>and</u> their loved ones - is regularly overlooked. A wedding rite affords a profound opportunity for both collective celebration and deeply personal odyssey.

Meaning and Purpose of the Public Wedding Ceremony

Formal Acknowledgement and Public Commitment

A wedding ceremony provides the arena for a couple to publicly declare their choice of life partner. It is an opportunity to consecrate their intention, purpose and vision. It celebrates and anchors their love.

Externally honouring what we cherish in our hearts can be life-changing. A wedding ceremony is an outer expression of the commitment or spiritual bond that a couple have already made between themselves.

Blessing and Support

For me, the most compelling reason for getting married officially and publicly is to invite blessing - THE SUPPORT - of EVERYTHING from EVERYWHERE.

How exquisite to create an occasion to ask for help and support from all directions and all dimensions! Depending on a couple's worldview, a wedding ceremony can be an opportunity to call in ALL OF LIFE to bless, witness and guide them and their relationship.

The support of the seen and the unseen can be invoked. If your personal mythology includes God or holy beings, gods and goddesses, light beings, angels, guardians, or nature spirits - call on them. The qualities of the elements and the directions, the support and power of the rocks, trees, mountains, sea and sky can all be invited in. The spirit of land or place can be welcomed, thanked, and asked for blessing.

The Quaker wedding vow specifically calls on loved ones and 'Divine assistance' to support a couple in their marriage. Jewish lore teaches that when a couple unite, the whole of creation sings for them. Life itself rejoices at our acts and commitments of love. The invitation of a wedding ceremony (and every day!) is to receive the gifts that life wants to so abundantly bestow.

Robert Fulghum states that 'If the spirit of the wedding is right, then the entire service becomes a prayer for the bride and groom and all their friends and relatives to live in harmony with great and eternal truths.'[4]

We *need* the blessing of the community, our people. Everybody present forms the holding container of a marriage ceremony - a physical presence and force through which love and good wishes can flow. This fuels the strength and confidence of a union, extending into the marriage beyond and, having shared the wedding, increases the chances of support when difficulties arise.

We can also lean into the blessings of our ancestors, both personal and collective. Marriage is an ancient rite containing the power and wisdom of those who have walked it before us.

Witness

Another key point of a wedding rite is that the truths of our hearts are communicated in the presence of others. There is something pivotal about being seen, heard and affirmed within the formal context of ritual. Declaring ourselves before our community holds us accountable. Being

---

[4] *Robert Fulghum - 'From Beginning to End: The Rituals of Our Lives' (1995)*

witnessed grounds an intention, lending it great power and resolve.

The act of witnessing itself is not passive. As the celebrant[5], I remind guests of their invaluable role as both Witness and Support to the marriage taking place. I invite them to be fully present as *participants,* not as spectators of something from which they are separate, but as co-creators of a transformative life event. Guests can then feel they are a very real and intimate part of a couple's decision, making the occasion even more powerful for all present.

Threshold and Transition-Marker, Initiation

In many times and cultures, marriage transitioned a child into adulthood. Formal marriage often sanctioned sexual relations and allowed a couple to forge their own life, distinct from their family of origin.

Although this aspect of a marriage rite may no longer apply, ritually honouring a relationship still signifies a new chapter of life. Marianne Williamson[6] names a wedding as a time to encourage forgiveness of past transgressions in order to enter marriage reborn.

Strength and courage are often needed to reach the threshold of marriage, the altar of the heart. It may require significant maturation to embrace the demands of conscious union.

Initiation, by its very nature, includes both loss and gain. Stepping into the new often demands increasing our capacities and responsibilities at the expense of old ways

---

[5] *As inspired by Robert Fulghum above*
[6] *Marianne Williamson (b. 1952) - American spiritual leader, activist, and author.*

of being. Relinquishing the familiar can be difficult and may feel like the death that is required to give birth to the new.

Transformation

The sorts of transformations made possible through the rite of marriage are numerous. The obvious external one is of change of status; from being unmarried to married, perhaps assuming a different surname or the title of husband or wife.

Internally, there may be subtle or overt shifts in the way we feel about ourselves and each other. There might be a sense of maturation, or of having been 'claimed,' or something 'settling' inside. For others, it might be a feeling of 'home-coming,' or a greater sense of belonging, or purpose, or deepening.

Ritual can lead us into realms of mystery, wonderment, reverence…

For many, getting married represents the rare occasion where we are given permission to shine bright and be celebrated for it. We are Queen and King for a day, God and Goddess.

We recognise and celebrate the best in each other.

Affirming Community, Family, and Kinship Ties

Traditionally, marriage has never been an isolated event involving only two individuals. It's a change that impacts social relationships, status and perhaps, even the infrastructure of a whole community. When two people marry, they become part of the same family. Their bloodlines merge; they inherit one another's ancestors and form their own branch of the family tree.

Drawing on her West African heritage, Sobonfu Somé[7] writes of the vitality and inter-weaving of an individual marriage within the context of the whole web of life. She teaches that 'a wedding is an opportunity - an obligation almost - for everyone to reaffirm relationships with one another, with the ancestors, with all the things around. So the wedding is not just a matter between two people but an event with a purpose for everyone in the village.'[8]

A wedding marks a change of status for everybody and helps everyone see and feel their place within a new constellation. A family gains a new member. A parent may feel the loss of a child, even if they still see them regularly. A friendship may receive a different kind of attention. Priorities and loyalties may change.

Wedding as GIFT to ALL Present

If we fully *include ourselves* in a ritual experience, we are all enriched. Our lives become more whole and real. If we deeply connect - with ourselves, with others, with Source – a wedding can be heart and soul medicine. This can be true for the couple, the guests, the community, the planet, and even for past and future generations.

A wedding reminds us to realign the focus of our lives on love. It offers a communal opportunity for pause and reflection on the things that matter. It invites the practice of gratitude alongside the grieving of losses inherent to loving. Grief and praise; a powerful teaching at the core of what it means to be fully human.[9]

---

[7] *Sobonfu Somé (d. 2017) – of the Dagara people of Burkina Faso, Some brought her West African heritage and teachings to the West.*

[8] *Sobonfu Somé - 'The Spirit of Intimacy' (1997)*

[9] *Inspired by teachings of Martin Prechtel in 'The Smell of Rain on Dust: Grief and Praise' (2015)*

Witnessing a couple state their vows allows everyone to connect with the love and goodness in their life, however it shows up. It gives space for yearnings and longing to breathe. It invites other couples to consciously reinvigorate their own wedding vows and marriages.

Wedding as Template for the Marriage

If the spirit of a wedding is clearly focused on love, abundance, and joy, this can establish the foundations of the life to come. If the wedding day is 'life distilled into a single, and singular event,'[10] then every detail of the planning, and the event itself, become imbued with special significance.

Even if things do not quite go to plan, when the important things are intact and a couple are connected to the meaning of their marriage, they can meet anything with humour and grace.

In Praise of Marriage

Now shall your heart be forever with my heart
Now shall your arms be forever my home
Lyrics from a song by Brendan Taaffe[11]

The marriage being celebrated here is based on love, mutual growth, happiness, and shared purpose. Viewing

---

[10] *Philip Zaleski and Paul Kaufman - 'Gifts of the Spirit: Living the Wisdom of the Great Religious Traditions' (1998)*
[11] *I love to sing this song! Words by Brendan Taaffe, a US songster, he wrote it for friends getting married, based on a Macedonian folk tune.*

intimate relationships as a vehicle for healing and transformation changes everything.

In fashioning a model of marriage that supports and inspires, we can no longer be bound by the institutions of the past. We can carry forward, or adapt, anything that is helpful, but whatever we create has to serve life.

Marianne Williamson teaches that marriage is 'not an escape from the world, but a commitment to greater service to it.'[12] It is an agreement between two people that serves their soul's growth and their highest good. Whenever we heal or grow, overcome blocks to love, or act with kindness and compassion – we serve life.

A friend told me once that one of the hexagrams of the *I Ching* (a divinatory tool of ancient China) depicts intimate relationship as two birds flying together in formation. And, most importantly, if a feather – one single feather – falls from either bird, it floats to the ground as a blessing.

Another version of the powerful marriage that serves the world is offered by story-teller Martin Shaw: 'The deep wedding is where the beloveds stand *back to back* with each other, facing outwards towards the world not just hypnotised in each other's gaze. It's a marriage that reaches out, raises up, blesses the crops, the curly-headed toddlers, to steady the infirm and sorrowful of heart.'[13]

Marriage as Container and Healing Ground

Foundations of trust and safety are essential for healing and transformation to take place. The act of marriage creates a powerful and protective holding container for this,

---

[12] *Marianne Williamson – 'A Return to Love' (1992)*
[13] *Martin Shaw - 'All Those Barbarians' (2020)*

precisely because of the commitment to life together <u>come what may.</u> Something is created which is far greater than the two individuals involved.

This is love in action: the willingness 'TO TAKE EACH OTHER ON no holds barred,'[14] that we may grow into fuller and fuller versions of ourselves. This is only made possible through EACH OTHER and THE CRUCIBLE OF OUR RELATIONSHIPS. Having someone at our side gives us a profound opportunity to heal anything that hinders our capacity to love.

Love brings up EVERYTHING that is not itself in order that we may heal beyond it. The inevitable hurts we experience in our lives can shut us down, harden our hearts, or make us angry and afraid. Our experiences and conditioning colour our ability to give and receive love. In fact, they impact how intimate and present we can be.

All of this, we bring to our partnerships, including the most tumultuous and challenging patterns of behaviour. To hold and withstand this, the container must be strong.

It takes time, energy, goodwill and fortitude to build and sustain such a container. Some places we can only go because of the trusted presence of our chosen loved one. The container that we create together needs to handle fire. And be as soft as feather down. As flexible as it is firm. And as steeped in kindness as it is anchored in integrity.

It is wild paradox that loving another can make us so vulnerable and yet be our greatest salvation too. If a marriage has strong roots, we can be haven one to

---

[14] *John Welwood - 'Journey of the Heart - The Path of Conscious Love'*
(1990)

another. It can be a place of home-coming. Home for the heart.

Marriage as a Path or Practice

Re-visioning marriage as a sacred path, or way of being, breathes new energy into it. It expresses something of the journey and potential of a conscious partnership. Put slightly differently, marriage can be 'a lifelong search for holiness in the context of domestic life.'[15]

Remembering the sacred nature of marriage is particularly helpful at times of struggle or conflict. When we truly 'show up' with each other, no matter how messy, this is us *doing the work* - the good, vital, heart-and-soul work of being human.

Of course, the Path of Marriage and Intimacy also contains many delights. Joy, companionship, healing, warmth, fulfilment, ecstasy, stability, tenderness, fun - all these and more may be ours along the way. Perhaps it is for this that marriage is called 'The Path of Beauty' by some First Nation's peoples.

Our loving matters. And requires as much dedication as any other spiritual practice.

Individual Inner Work

Relationships can only flourish when we, as individuals, take full responsibility for our personal healing and well-being. The work is inner, and always we must return to our primary intimacy - the relationship we have with ourselves.

---

[15] *Dr. Petroc Willey as quoted in 'Gifts of the Spirit: Living the Wisdom of the Great Religious Traditions' by Zaleski and Kaufmann*

We can only ever be as loving, kind, generous and compassionate to another as we are able to be with ourselves. The work of the 'inner marriage' is a call to wholeness, embracing and reconciling all of the opposites - masculine/feminine, shadow/light - that are contained within us all, regardless of gender or of having a partner.

Marriage as Prayer

Through devotion to a chosen partner, all of life can be praised. Living an intimate relationship can become a prayer. What if we related to existence from the knowledge that we have married an aspect of the divine?

How we cherish and honour our life partner (and our children, and our friends…) serves, in parallel, a love much greater than ourselves that is way beyond the personal.

The most powerful prayer is the one that gives thanks. We can, for example, wake each morning aware of the miraculous gift of sharing our life with another. Love and Gratitude are inextricably entwined. In a life-generating cycle, the loving heart automatically gives thanks and rejoices, while gratitude in the heart creates more love.

In our contemporary bid for independence and autonomy, coupled with a focus on material 'success,' it can be easy to lose sight of the mystery and wonder of life and one another.

Many of us have forgotten the wide potential of the power of love. Let us not underestimate how we can impact our own spheres of influence.

In a life-rejoicing partnership, both the bride and groom are fulfilled. When She is truly seen, honoured and adored by Him, alchemy takes place. His love and devotion opens her

(her greatest longing), and he is showered effortlessly with her abundant love. This is *his* deepest longing.

And Finally...

One simple answer to the complex question 'Why marry?:'[16]

It's so much friendlier with two

---

[16] *From 'Winnie-The-Pooh' by A. A. Milne, illustrated by E. H. Shepard, which inspired the order of service at Cath & Andy's wedding, 2009*

CHAPTER TWO

The Power of Ritual

Ceremonies transcend the boundaries of the individual and resonate beyond the human realm.
Robin Wall Kimmerer in 'Braiding Sweetgrass'

Ritual has always been an integral part of human existence. People once knew that it's what makes life *work,* forming the bedrock of a healthy, happy and connected community. We do not thrive without it, and a sense of purpose, belonging, and intimacy are hard to establish and maintain as our everyday reality and birthright.

Ritual is strong medicine. It is soul work. It offers an 'out of ordinary' experience where we can commune with our 'vast' selves, with the parts of us that know and that can dream, vision and see. Sacred space is the container of raw power. Its purpose is transformation. From this place, we align with the mystery that is life itself, the very fabric of the universe.

I believe this was once known intimately and corresponds with our primal expectations of belonging and being cherished. To unfathomable detriment, we have largely lost the 'language' of ritual, the way of praise, of grieving cleanly and the means of connecting powerfully to Source/God.

The decline of ritual initiation has taken place over centuries in the West. The Church held sway for hundreds of years, dispensing formulaic rituals which, while perhaps fulfilling an important social role, seldom had the power to transform. Our rituals have become watered down, our ceremonies diluted to a pale echo of what they once were and what they could be.

This loss and disconnection go largely unrecognised, as our roots in ritual have gone unnourished for generations. We may know nebulous aches and empty places that yearn things that have no names, as we long to be touched by the sacredness of life once more. We have grown unconfident, even ill at ease or afraid, in the primal ways of ritual.

We are starting to recognise the impact of this disempowerment and gradually beginning to reclaim something of our heritage. Let us not hesitate to come together in celebration of life's joys and passages.

'Ritual' and 'Ceremony'

Some believe that all religious rites began with the celebration of menstruation. Ancient cultures considered menstrual blood most sacred as it was associated with the potential for new life.

Another suggestion links 'ritual' with an Indo-European root meaning 'to fit together.' This suggests a weaving and bringing together of many parts - the seen and the unseen, the tangible and intangible, matter and spirit - to create a fuller picture, with healing at its core.

The word 'ceremony' comes from Old French, via the original Latin *caerimonia,* which conveys a sense of sacredness, awe and a reverent rite. It suggests an invitation to put everyday busyness aside, to come inwards and 'home.' To enter the realms of transcendence.

Nowadays, the term 'ceremony' and 'ritual' are often used interchangeably. However, 'There is a seismic difference between a rite-of-passage 'ceremony' and a rite-of-passage process or 'ritual.' A ceremony that marks the beginning or the completion of a rite of passage is different from a ritual that actually instigates and contains a person's transformative experience.'[17]

It is important to differentiate between these two types of ritual-ceremonial event:

1. Those that mark or celebrate a transition that has *already* occurred.

2. Those designed to *bring* about a desired change of status or perception.

A wedding rite may contain elements of both.

> *Ceremony focuses attention so that attention becomes intention.*
> Robin Wall Kimmerer in 'Braiding Sweetgrass'

The Role of Ritual

To reiterate: ritual is essentially about TRANSFORMATION. A ritual that does not bring about some shift has not served its purpose. It provides a structure where change can take place.

---

[17] *Zia Ali - an Interfaith Minister peer*

We cross a threshold and transition from one state of being to another. By necessity, this signifies both an ending and a beginning.

Ritual is an outward manifestation of an inner decision or intention. It is an external event either facilitating or marking an internal shift. The Christian seven sacraments (of which marriage is one) are described as 'outward and visible signs of an inward and spiritual grace.' When conscious intent is focused on an act, the power of this act is magnified.

Whether subtle, dramatic, one-off or oft-repeated, effective ritual means that life will be different afterwards. Ritual welcomes us to align with cosmic strength and grace, 'handing over' to something greater than ourselves. Sometimes, *the transformative power is one of release, of being set free to become closer to our authentic selves.*

The sacred nature of ritual extends beyond the verbal. It bridges the ordinary and the extraordinary, the mundane and the profound. Through it, we access different ways of knowing and seeing via feelings, visions, intuition, the way the body wants to move, the sounds that may come from our throats, the colours from a paintbrush. We are offered the possibility of integration of all aspects of our being.

Rituals, ceremonies and festivals affirm our shared humanity.

Elements of Ritual Initiation

Anthropologists describe traditional rites of passage as consisting of three stages: separation, liminality, and re-integration. Let's explore these with specific reference to marriage and with the invitation to be curious about what each may mean for you.

Separation – stepping away from the familiar, from all that has been known and lived so far. This stage clearly marks that a phase of life has ended. It denotes the beginning of a new one. It involves a loss, a death of sorts, and an accompanying need to mourn (or at least to acknowledge). 'Yes' to one possibility means 'no' to another. Marriage signals the death of singledom and an end to the possibility of life with someone else.

Liminality[18] - this term comes from Latin *limin*, meaning 'threshold.' It marks the moment of crossing over, a 'betwixt and between' zone of being neither in the old state nor fully in the new.

This 'liminal' space includes the event itself and the necessary preparation beforehand. Because ritual evokes a change of consciousness, it needs to take place outside of ordinary life, in time and physical space set apart.

This can be a highly creative, expansive, and intuitive time of great gifts. It is a period of unformed but forming. It can feel like mapless territory - scary yet exciting - and a time for taking stock. There may be a sense of things growing, or of things falling away.

Re-integration - this phase marks the return to everyday life, but as someone who has experienced the inner and outer landscapes of a rite of passage *and been changed by them*. The new status of husband/wife is now inwardly and publicly known.

'Mapping' the Wedding Rite

When we appreciate that the wedding rite encompasses the *whole process of 'getting married,'* the possibility of

---

[18] *Anthropologist Victor Turner (1920-1983) coined the term 'liminal.'*

exploration and growth becomes more obvious. Solely understanding it as the 'official' day of ceremony and celebrations is a major disservice and dishonouring.

A couple enters the marriage ritual with the first 'Yes' of engagement. It continues through to the formal/legal /official/spiritual acknowledgement of crossing the threshold. It extends into the time of feasting and merry-making and, then, into the short transitioning period of what has traditionally been the honeymoon. The integration of what it means to 'be married' and settling and deepening into this change of being may continue indefinitely.

This period can be anything from a few days to months, and even years. I consider it all ritual - sacred - because it is no longer quite of the ordinary. Something gets set in motion; the intention of changing status is named but not yet realised. Once the threshold is crossed, it then takes time to register this transition.

To simplify, the wedding rite can be broken down into four distinct and universal elements:

1. Period of Preparation – the intent is known (time of betrothal or engagement)

2. Wedding Ceremony – the FORMAL marking of the marriage taking place

3. Celebration/Festivities – the INFORMAL marking of the marriage taking place

4. Period of Integration – recognising a threshold has been crossed (the honeymoon period, and beyond)

How we experience each of these stages is very individual. As well as anticipation and joy, we can also be confronted with fear or resistance on the journey from the initial agreement to marry to the formal wedding ceremony and on into married life.

The 'big day' itself can be anything from a five minute 'official' ceremony to several days' worth of communal involvement, which likely includes several related rituals. We remember again that all of it - including the feasting and merry-making, the camaraderie and jostling, the speeches and pranks - is ritual; 'time out of time,' not the everyday...

For the couple, this 'non-ordinary' state of being ideally extends into the honeymoon. This could be considered a 'ritual of return' in that it is time apart for the couple to start integrating the very new fact of their marriage. Gradually they can prepare to return to their everyday lives, 'the same, but different.'

Although the formal ceremony has ended, the process or 'invisible' workings may continue for much longer. Time is needed for integration.

> *Ceremonies have layers and, given a subtle blend of space and attention, they will speak to us over many cycles of moon and sun.*
> Mac Macartney from 'The Children's Fire: Heart Song of a People'

Marriage Archetypes

This small section touches on the inner work of entering the holy ground of marriage. At a fundamental level, the marriage rite recognises our essential goodness, beauty and loveability. For many, this can be difficult to accept. It can be a journey to claim ourselves in our fullness, knowing we are worthy of loving and being loved.

In folklore and tales, this process of 'becoming' is often represented by the archetypes of prince and princess, queen and king. Only when this status is reached can marriage take place.

In the stories, girls come to know their identity as a princess, boys as a prince. This is often a gradual, painful process as depicted, for example, in the fairy-tale 'Cinderella.' Here, the girl in ashes, treated as a slave, eventually becomes a princess, ready to meet her prince. Ugliness turns to beauty. Similarly, after harshness and endurance, the 'ugly duckling' in Hans Christian Anderson's tale sees himself as the stunning swan that he is.

When the time is right - after one hundred years of sleep, or 'impossible' tasks performed by the hero or heroine - the princess or prince will, with maturation, become Queen or King.

These tales teach of transformation and of daring to look, touch and even to kiss (as in the princess and the frog) the 'ugliness', the 'warts', the shame... INTO BEAUTY.

And then 'sovereignty' can emerge, as the *wholeness* of ourselves is now known and accepted.

Complexity

It is important to acknowledge the undercurrents, subtleties and complexities of relationship and emotion that are invariably present - yet often ignored - at any community and family gathering. Everything gets intensified by ritual and ceremony. Emotions are heightened as feelings run both deep and close to the surface.

Along with joy and happiness, more complex (and less socially acceptable...) feelings may arise, such as jealousy, grief, fear, loss or guilt. Family tensions can be hard to ignore.

Being aware of all of this gives us a framework of compassion, that the gifts of the occasion may be more fully received by everyone present.

CHAPTER THREE

A History of Marriage

Introduction

We may never fully know the history, customs and worldviews surrounding marriage rites of older times. It is likely they were long considered an essential fertility or coming-of-age rite. In one way or another, they have served to mark a major life transition while invoking guidance and protection.

When convenience, power, wealth, or status has been central, extensive wounding has also been inflicted in the name of marriage. As a legality protecting property and bloodline, principles such as love, happiness, fulfilment, higher purpose, or relationship as a spiritual path were of little consequence.

I want to give an overview of the fascinating story of marriage because it demonstrates how understandings and expectations can radically shift. In doing so, it may encourage us to utilise what nourishes and leave the rest. I am also interested in unearthing perspectives on this age-old rite that may spark joy and inspiration.

Marriage and the Feminine

In previous eras, women were revered for their capacity to bring forth life, and so marriage was naturally considered their domain. Therefore, the rituals surrounding it primarily focused on the bride's experience. Nature, the feminine, abundance, joy, and sexuality were central themes.

The rite was so life-changing for women because it marked their transition to mistress of hearth and home and their entrance into the life-threatening realms of childbirth. The Goddess was venerated (as opposed to a God or gods) and appealed to in all matters relating to marriage and family life.

The Latin *maritare* ('to marry') referred to a union overseen by the Goddess Aphrodite-Mari. Likewise, Juno, the Great Mother-Goddess of the Romans and the protector of the household and childbirth, guided every aspect of marriage through her priestesses.

June is named in her honour and was long the favourable month for weddings. Barbara Walker names some of her multiple aspects and roles:[19]

Juno Pronuba - arranged marriages
Juno Domiduca – led the bride across the threshold of her new home
Juno Nuxia – anointed the doorposts
Juno Cinxia – untied the bride's virgin-girdle
Juno Lucina – watched over her pregnancy
Juno Sospita – took care of her in labour
Juno Ossipago – strengthened her baby's bones
Juno Rumina – provided breast milk

---

[19] *Barbara G. Walker - 'The Woman's Encyclopedia of Myths and Secrets' (1983)*

In some times and cultures, a man was considered spiritually incomplete until he knew a woman intimately physically, thus linking him to the Goddess. This was his sole route to fully experiencing the divine. 'Hieros Gamos' (Greek for 'sacred union') was regarded as the holiest of acts, celebrating the sexual union between a woman and a man, whereby each became spiritually whole.

In Hinduism, the gods themselves had to be married, recognising that male spiritual authority depended on woman. Similarly, early Israelites could only become priests if they were married. Ancient Germanic cultures revered the life-giving nature of the feminine, and tantra teaches that every woman is the Goddess personified, an aspect of Life itself.

A woman's direct and powerful link with the life cycle gave her complete autonomy in the home. A Hindu scripture names the wife as 'House-Goddess,' and generally, a husband 'should never punish his wife, but should cherish her... By riches, clothes, love, respect and pleasing words should one's wife be satisfied.'

The Shift from Matriarchy to Patriarchy

In the Western world, the shift in the power balance between the sexes happened gradually and in direct correlation to the accumulation of property and wealth. As settled life replaced nomadism, houses were built and land was acquired, becoming valuable assets to pass on to the next generation. This meant more to defend in times of attack and, as men predominantly took on this role, the matriarchal society and worldview became subsumed by the patriarchal one.

Walker writes of myths recording 'the transition from loose, flexible marital arrangements favoured by Goddesses to the rigid monogamy favoured by Gods.'[20] Wives had to be faithful and obedient and lost their status. Christianity later followed suit, and similar changes happened in the parts of India where monogamy was adopted.

Christianity and Marriage

Early Christianity was hostile towards marriage, women, sexuality, motherhood and family life in general. It saw all these as degrading 'spirituality,' beginning the devastating rift between sexuality and spirituality from which we still suffer today. The Church only began to take control of the institution of marriage when power and wealth became of bigger concern, and the rite gradually became formalised and prescriptive.

The Church's opposition to marriage was also originally so strong because the Goddess was so prominent. As Walker candidly put it, Christianity in the end only accepted marriage 'on the condition that a slave/master relationship was formed and that the Goddess, whose many forms had protected the married woman in all phases of matrimony and motherhood, was eliminated.'[21]

She also noted that 'the idea that a male priest preside alone over a marriage ceremony was unthinkable – which is one reason why Christians didn't think of it.' This explains why marriage remained under the jurisdiction of common law for centuries. In essence, wedding rites were traditional

[20] *Barbara G. Walker - 'The Woman's Encyclopedia of Myths and Secrets' (1983)*

[21] *Barbara G. Walker - 'The Woman's Encyclopedia of Myths and Secrets' (1983)*

folk ceremonies dating back to pagan times. ('Pagan' simply means 'country,' the village folk who lived close to the cycles of nature). The ritual of secular toasts, vows, feasting and merry-making with the whole village was what mattered.

Marriage contracts centred around the Viking concept of 'the morning gift' (*morgengifu*), which was given to the wife by her new husband the morning after their wedding night. This could be substantial amounts of land or money. Old English law protected women, supporting their ownership of property and land. Christianity revoked the law, not only placing a wife's property in her husband's hands, but herself becoming his property, devoid of rights.

The common law vows, still recognisable today, were concerned with transferring stewardship of a woman's land to her 'houseman' (husband). A groom vowed: 'With this ring I thee wed and this gold and silver I give thee and with my body I thee worship, and with all my worldly chattels I thee honour.' The bride answered: 'I take thee to be my wedded husband, to have and to hold, for fairer for fouler, for better for worse, for richer for poorer, in sickness and in health, to be bonny and buxom in bed and at board, till death us depart.'

The Church's earliest acknowledgement of marriage was a simple blessing held '*outside the church's closed doors* to keep the pollution of lust out of God's house.'[22] By popular demand, the custom became legal in 1215, despite it technically breaking church law. Marriage only became one of the Christian 'Seven Sacraments' in the fifteenth century.

---

[22] *Barbara G. Walker - 'The Woman's Encyclopedia of Myths and Secrets'* *(1983)*

In the sixteenth century, as the Church took greater and greater control, it became a legal requirement to be married by a priest in a consecrated church. By this time, a wife had no legal rights and could own nothing. Children born out of wedlock were considered illegitimate for the first time.

Wedding values and traditions will have varied greatly amongst rich and poor and between rural and urban areas. Common-law marriages tended to be informal. Indeed, under country law that was still officially practised until the Church forbade it in 1563, marriages 'could be freely initiated and terminated without formality by either party and at any time.'[23] In addition, trial marriages were legal until the early 1800s. In Scotland, non-church related weddings were legal right up until 1939.

'Romantic Love'

Weddings have often essentially been business contracts between parents, regardless of the wishes of the wedding pair themselves. This was the basis of marriage for thousands of years across the globe and, in many cultures, still is.[24]

Writer Elizabeth Gilbert differentiates between these 'pragmatic marriages' and those based on love and emotional connection. In the former, 'the interests of the larger community are considered above the interests of the two individuals involved.'[25] We now highlight the difference

---

[23] *Barbara G. Walker - 'The Woman's Encyclopedia of Myths and Secrets' (1983)*

[24] *Worldwide, over 50% of marriages today are still arranged.*

[25] *Elizabeth Gilbert - 'Committed' (2010), famously the author of 'Eat, Pray, Love'*

between a sense of '*You* matter' ('romantic') as opposed to 'your *role* matters' ('pragmatic').

Romantic weddings are very recent, although notions of 'romantic love' and chivalry date from twelfth-century Europe. When we understand that expectations of personal happiness within marriage were not the norm, we can begin to appreciate how significant these concepts have been on our contemporary views on relationships and marriage.

It is shocking to realise that the Christian church, among others, even sanctioned 'chastisement' of wives by husbands. Marital violence and abuse were so standard that no woman was expected to love her husband. The term 'lover' referred to a man outside the marriage.

Stephanie Coontz summarised this position when she wrote that 'most societies have had romantic love, this combination of sexual passion, infatuation, and the romanticization of the partner. But very often, those things were seen as inappropriate when attached to marriage. Because marriage was a political, economic, and mercenary event, many people believed that true, uncontaminated love could only exist without it.'[26]

Some Dates and Perspectives

- Early Greek and Roman cultures feared female sexuality, whereas the Celts, Norse, Saxons and Normans naturally embraced it.

- In ancient times, couples in a sexual relationship could be legally married simply by declaring themselves so.

---

[26] *Stephanie Coontz, as quoted in Esther Perel 'The State of Affairs; Rethinking Infidelity' (2017)*

No witness, priest, nor formality were required. Couples often pledged themselves to one another at secret sacred sites, particular to each locality. In Britain, these tended to be waterfalls, standing stones, or ancient trees, especially the oak.

- Viking and Celtic weddings were held outside. Everything important happened outdoors - in full view and witnessed by the gods - and this was common practice up to the sixteenth century. Marriage, often in the form of a handfasting rite, was deeply sacred within Druidism. Roman weddings were still essentially nature-based, while Saxon marriage rites emphasised fertility. By Norman times, the virginity of the bride was considered most significant.

- Poorer folk of the British Isles often marked marriage informally and may have used the gatherings at the eight annual seasonal festivals to announce and celebrate a wedding. Both Beltane (1st May) and Lammas (early August) were particularly associated with marriage.

- Scottish marriage laws have always been more relaxed than the English. The age of consent, for instance, was lower in Scotland, and marriage there did not require parental consent. The Marriage Act of 1753 required parental approval for English couples under 21, and a marriage had to be publicly announced in case of objection. Meanwhile, in Scotland, girls over 12 and boys over 14 could get married simply by declaring vows in front of witnesses. Anybody could perform a marriage, and anyone present would bear witness.

This has meant that, for several hundred years (right up until 1940), secret 'runaway' weddings have been performed for

English couples just over the border in Scotland. Gretna Green, less than a mile into Scotland, became the most famous elopement destination.

Runaway weddings typically took place in inns, blacksmith's cottages or the forge itself, where the rings were made. Blacksmiths performing ceremonial duties became so prevalent it gave rise to the term 'blacksmith' or 'anvil weddings.' Unofficial weddings have been called 'blacksmith weddings' since the 1500s. In reality, however, anyone could take the role, and some – like the local fisherman, weaver, cobbler or mole catcher – would have been less costly than the highly regarded blacksmith.

The officiant of an 'anvil wedding' typically ended the ceremony by striking the anvil, representing a union as durable as a blacksmith fusing metal.

- In many faiths and countries, it has been the age-old norm to celebrate a wedding over several days. In general, Christianity has vehemently disapproved of the strong, wild folk spirit that makes merry with such joy and freedom.

- The romantic white wedding considered 'traditional' today only came in the nineteenth century, popularised by Queen Victoria.

- 1837 - Civil marriage was introduced in England. Couples could now be legally married outside the Church of England, in a registry office.

- 2005 - Same-sex civil partnerships became legal in the UK.

- 2014 - Same-sex civil marriages became legal in the UK.

- Interracial marriage was ILLEGAL in the USA - the laws only started changing around this in 1967. The same was true in South Africa until apartheid ended.

Marriage in the Dominant Culture West Today

Perspectives on marriage have never shifted more dramatically than over the last fifty years or so. As we've seen, marriage has gradually evolved from an economic arrangement of duty and obligation to one of love and care that is freely chosen.

Feminism, contraception and abortion rights have radically changed women's lives. With divorce a viable option, author Perel[27] noted that if women now '*could* leave, they needed a better reason to stay. Henceforward, the bar of marital quality had been raised significantly-'

Perel eloquently describes this shift: 'First we brought love to marriage. Then we brought sex to love. Then we linked marital happiness with sexual satisfaction. Sex for procreation gave way to sex for recreation. While premarital sex became the norm, marital sex underwent its own little revolution, shifting from a woman's matrimonial duty to a joint pathway for pleasure and connection.'

She goes on to say that 'Never before have our expectations of marriage taken on such epic proportions. We still want everything the traditional family was meant to provide - security, children, property, and respectability - but now we also want our partner to love us, to desire us, to be *interested* in us. We should be best friends, trusted confidants, and passionate lovers to boot...'

---

[27] *Esther Perel - 'The State of Affairs: Rethinking Infidelity' (2017)*

It is a lot to ask, and yet let us celebrate the potential of the monumental shift this represents. From originating as a women's rite of protection and blessing, marriage has evolved through patriarchal times into a wealth-focused contract, into today's era where love and happiness are central. We can now witness the freedom and joy available to two equally invested individuals co-creating a profound and beautiful wedding ceremony as a foundation to their thriving marriage.

CHAPTER FOUR

Wedding Words and their Origins

While researching this book, I became fascinated with the origins of words associated with marriage. In some cases, the original sacred meaning has been obscured or lost, so shedding light may offer new perspectives and the possibility of reclaiming and healing. Other words are listed for interest or to celebrate where we have moved beyond the original meaning in ways that promote dignity, respect and wholeness.

'Marriage'

'Marriage' comes from the Latin *maritare,* linking us to the Goddess Aphrodite-Mari, who was the protectress of the union of marriage.

The more archaic 'matrimony' is derived from the Latin word for mother (*mater*). *Matrimony* therefore emphasises what was considered the key purpose of marriage.

Other languages tell different stories:

- *Kiddushin* - the Hebrew word for marriage translates as 'sanctification,' implying a sacred commitment.

- 'Path of Beauty' - describes marriage within some indigenous American traditions.

- *Брак ('brak')* - this Russian word has the verb 'to take' as its root, likely referring to the ancient practice of bride kidnapping.

'Wedding'

This comes from the Anglo-Saxon *wed,* meaning pledge. Couples were sometimes betrothed as children, a 'wed' being given to the future bride to secure the agreement.

- *Anand Karaj* - the Sikh word describes a wedding as a 'blissful event.'

- *Свадьба ('Svadba')* - literally meaning 'connection of families,' the Russian term emphasises the uniting of two families.

- *Die Hochzeit* - the German equivalent translates as 'High Time,' signifying an event of special importance.

'Man'/'Woman'

Etymology connects 'woman' with 'moon.' The Indo-European *man* (referring to a woman) meant both 'moon' and 'wisdom.' A man was a *wer (*as in *wer-wulf;* a man-wolf).

By the time of Anglo-Saxon English, the term *mann* referred to both sexes. Women and men were now defined by their roles: men were 'weaponed-persons' *(waepnedmenn)*, while women were 'wife-persons' *(wifmenn)* connected to the word for 'weaving.'

'Bride'/'Bridegroom'

Some suggest that the word 'bride' comes from the most revered Celtic Goddess of the British Isles - Brigit, Bridget,

Brige, Bride. Our concept of bride, then, is linked to the great Goddess herself. On his wedding day, man marries an aspect of the Goddess, in human female form. He, as the bride's groom, is the servant of the Goddess.

'Husband'/'Wife'

When property rights were matrilineal, the word husband referred to 'one bonded to the house.' He tended his wife's land and animals, giving rise to the term 'husbandry.' The word described his role, defined by his relation to the feminine (both the Earth as goddess, and woman as the goddess personified). He was 'husbandman' or guardian to Her.

Folklore abounds with this motif. Her warriors and guardians have included Morris men and the Oak and Holly Kings, who battled out the ancient seasonal rites to tend to her over summer and winter. These masculine figures are all the god personified and essential in their service to the feminine. One cannot survive without the other.

'Wife' derives from the Anglo-Saxon *wifmann,* 'weaving person'; a role typically designated to women.

'Spouse'

This outdated description of a marriage partner comes from a Latin root combining the idea of binding oneself formally to another by performing a rite.

In Russian, the term has the same root as the words for 'harness' and 'team of horses,' signifying two people linked together, sharing the same load.

'Hen' and 'Stag' Parties

There is some debate about the origins of the names of these rites. Some languages emphasise the all-male or all-female aspect of the occasion, while others highlight the life transition it marks:

- The terms 'Stag' and 'Hen,' referring to the soon-to-be groom and bride, originated in Britain and are now common in Ireland and Canada also. In fourteenth-century English, the words referred to the male and female of any species and gradually became slang for 'man' and 'woman' too.

Another theory suggests the word 'hen' comes from 'hinnie' or 'hennie,' meaning 'honey.' 'Hen' is still used as a term of endearment in northern Britain.

Furthermore, in Scotland, the women gathered in advance for 'the hen wedding,' to pluck numerous chickens in preparation for the coming feast.

The noble 'stag' likely links with the ancient Celtic god Cernunnos, also known as Herne the Hunter. He was a horned God, representing the divine masculine and connected to sexuality and the life cycle.

- 'Buck' and 'Hen' - Australia, with a British English influence.

- Bachelor/Bachelorette Parties – US. *Bachelor* originally meant a 'young knight-in-training' but came to mean an unmarried man by the fourteenth century.

- *'Addio al celibato/nubilato'* - Italy, translates as 'Farewell to bachelor/maidenhood.'

- *'Junggesellenabschied'* - like the Italian, the German equivalent expresses a 'farewell' to youth.

- '*Enterrement de vie de garçon/jeune ville*' - France, translates as the 'burial/funeral of life as a boy/girl.'

- '*Malchishnik/Devichnik*' - Russia, roughly translating as 'boys'/girls' party.'

- Contemporary times have introduced the concept of 'stag and doe', or 'hag' parties (combining 'hen' and 'stag'), where bride and groom celebrate this pre-wedding rite together.

- 'Last Night of Freedom' has also been a popular term for these events for both groom and bride-to-be.

'Vow'

This comes from the Latin verb 'to promise.'

'Betrothed'

This word has 'truth' at its heart *(troth),* linked to *bi-* meaning 'thoroughly'. It conveys a full commitment to one's promise.

'Confetti'

I believe this comes from the Italian tradition of giving wedding guests sugared almonds ('il confetto'). As well as symbolising fertility, this original 'confetti' was a metaphor for the joys and sorrows of life, as represented by the slightly bitter nut coated in sugar.

'To Celebrate'

This is derived from an ancient Greek root meaning 'to sing, dance, praise.'

'To Consecrate'

This means to make sacred. It implies setting a conscious intention(s) from a place of reverence and gratitude to something greater than ourselves.

'To Respect'

From the Latin *respicere* meaning 'to gaze at,' this conveys a sense of being fully seen and known.

CHAPTER FIVE

Some Reflections on Vows

Not all cultures include the speaking of formal vows to transition a couple across the threshold of marriage. Set rites that are culturally known and recognised may often bind a couple. Within Hinduism, for example, completion of the 'Seven Steps' signifies that a couple is married, while Sikhs recite specific verses and circle their 'Holy Book' four times.

Yet in Western cultures, vows are at the heart of a wedding ceremony. A vow encapsulates both our highest intention and is the ground from which all else comes. They act almost as a magic formula, the 'abracadabra' moment, before which a couple is not quite married. And after which; they are married.

Whether understood as intentions, statements, declarations or promises, vows express a condensed vision of the marriage to follow. Simply put, they are each couple's version of 'this is what we want to say to each other, and this is the time to do it.'

An Eastern adage reminds us that *'You are much more likely to hit the target if you aim at it.'* The process of articulating a vision, writing it down and voicing it helps it become a lived reality. 'Name it and claim it' as one author exhorts.[28] The ancients knew that the power of our thoughts effects change, as science now supports.

> *Our intentions tend to bend our lives in the direction of those very intentions.*
> Stephen Cope in 'Deep Human Connection'

Marriage gives love form, providing a framework in which we can bring the totality of ourselves into alignment with our highest intention. Vows formally create a sacred space or alchemical vessel where the true and deep work of love and transformation can most effectively and safely take place.

Vows are not just words uttered once and agreed to on a solitary occasion. They are energies and have a life or spirit of their own. Like all living things, they grow and require nurturing. Frequent remembering is what strengthens them.

It is our willingness to do this that matters. Love is the fuel. Acts of kindness, caring, extending, forgiveness and understanding all breathe life into a vow. The words then become *inhabited*, converting into a tangible, lived reality.

> *Gonna walk this road, See where it leads*
> *Gonna bless the flowers, Gonna bless the weeds…*
> Lyrics from a song by Eric Bibb

---

[28] *Stephen Cope - 'Deep Human Connection: Why We Need It More Than Anything Else' (2019)*

The process of formulating a vow or truly engaging with pre-existing ones can be profound. It invites us to connect with what matters most and surrender to that. Norman Fischer describes making a vow as 'the experience of receiving an inner calling and answering that calling with your whole life.'[29]

Importantly, vows, unlike goals, can never be fully met all of the time. Vows *are* hard to keep, yet they serve as a steadfast touchstone, an anchor, a place to return to. Again quoting Fischer, vows are like 'walking toward the horizon: you know where you are headed, you can see the destination brightly up ahead, and you keep on going toward it with enthusiasm even though you never arrive there.'[30]

Cultural myth may talk of 'happily ever after,' but in truth, we can never know what will unfold. We can commit to meeting life together to the best of our ability and, when we fall, our vows can support us in moving forward. A Zen teaching uses the example of falling to the ground and needing the ground to push ourselves up again. Vows offer us a way of each taking responsibility to return the relationship to a safe, loving place once more.

When we vow - articulating our intentions - we open ourselves to help from somewhere beyond ourselves: a bigger, wider connection with all of creation. This connection can be our constant renewal, our vows endless inspiration.

---

[29] *Norman Fischer - 'Taking Our Places: The Buddhist Path to Truly Growing Up'*
[30] *Norman Fischer - 'Taking Our Places: The Buddhist Path to Truly Growing Up'*

Notes

♡ It is worth considering including an expression of love and commitment to any children of the union. This is especially pertinent if they are from previous relationships.

♡ I believe it is very powerful if a couple declare THEMSELVES married. We are so accustomed to being 'pronounced' married by somebody external to the relationship (a priest or other officiant) that we may forget that it ideally expresses our own sense of having crossed a threshold.

Fulghum[31] describes such an occasion when he officiated an intimate wedding on a beach. At the relevant point in the ceremony, the couple took themselves to the sea for a private moment. Once ready, they returned - declaring themselves married. The threshold moment had happened for them, in the privacy and presence of their own selves, the sea, the sky and the Great Mystery.

Examples

Here are two sets of personally-created vows, which speak of vision way beyond (but including) the happiness of the individual couple. The first are those spoken by two very dear friends, the second an excerpt from a book:

♥ I vow to be honest and true, taking responsibility for all that I feel and keeping the space between us clear so that love can flow.

---

[31] *Robert Fulghum - 'From Beginning to End: The Rituals of our Lives' (1995)*

I vow to be committed to you for the length of our journey together, standing behind you in support, walking beside you in friendship and holding your hand wherever the road may lead us.

I vow to honour and cherish all that you have been and all that you are and to offer you the freedom to grow into all you are becoming.

I vow to remember that our relationship is a gift and willingly surrender it to the greater purpose of Love.[32]

♥ We vow to uphold our togetherness, walking hand in hand through life, committed to working through our challenges and towards our dreams. We vow to cultivate harmony in our relationship, realising that nothing is more important than this, not even being right. We vow to honour one another, serve one another, and assist one another in bringing that which dwells in the kingdom of our heart, outward to the earth.[33]

---

[32] *Nickie & Neil - with kind permission, married on 7/01/2019*
[33] *Abridged from Caroline & Charles Muir's Wedding Vows in 'Tantra Goddess: A Memoir of Sexual Awakening' (2011)*

CHAPTER SIX

Honouring Sexuality within Intimate Relationship

Many old ways of being, thinking and doing have repressed our natural vibrancy and life force when it comes to our physical body, our sexuality and our love-making.

Our legacy around sexuality includes staggering shame and inhibition. However, we are beginning to explore new ways which celebrate the body. They are healing the ancient split between our body and mind, matter and spirit, feminine and masculine.

Andrew Harvey[34] passionately addresses both the wounding and an alternative paradigm when he teaches: 'It is lethal and obscene to keep alive the old patriarchal fears about sexuality. What is needed is for the body to be blessed. Why? Because we're in it. Why would we be here if we were not meant to love and celebrate our bodies…? When you finally learn how to love and celebrate your body and your sexuality, it's then that the full miracle of life becomes obvious to you.'

---

[34] *Andrew Harvey (b.1952) - British author, scholar and teacher of mystic traditions*

It is time to listen to our life-gifted beautiful bodies, capable of SO much beauty, healing, joy and tenderness. This is our birthright. Unencumbered by conditioning, we intrinsically know how to love - freely, openly, generously - in ways which infuse our whole beings with profound well-being.

This may not be the path for everyone. We each have our own ways of bringing love, blessing, and gratitude to life. Here, in relation to marriage, I celebrate the view that sexuality is sacred. In this context, physical intimacy is revered as a pathway to greater wholeness, serving not only the individuals involved but the whole planet.

The tantric master Barry Long[35] taught that 'The cause of most of the unhappiness on this earth is that man and woman have actually forgotten how to make physical love. This is the greatest tragedy of all time.' He reflected on 'how little satisfying sex is being enjoyed on Earth.'[36]

This is an urgent wake-up call. We can bestow so much kindness with and through our physical bodies. This is a form of communication that can restore and create peace, enhancing inner balance, harmony and joy between partners. For Barry Long, 'making love rightly' was his primary spiritual practice.

These ideas are becoming more widespread. Sex now becomes about transformation rather than simple physical gratification. It serves love. Being a conscious lover means being 'fully present with no agenda other than to give and receive love.'[37]

---

[35] *Barry Long (1926-2003) - an Australian writer and spiritual master*

[36] *Barry Long - 'Making Love: Sexual Love the Divine Way' (1988)*

[37] *Caroline Muir - 'Tantra Goddess: A Memoir of Sexual Awakening' (2011)*

Instead of being goal-oriented or lost in fantasy, relaxing and being alive to each moment can transform sex into a healing, creative, spiritual force. This generates vitality and energy rather than depleting it. It leads to peace rather than frustration and contributes to a life-enhancing change of consciousness.

This is radically different from the dominant-culture messages we currently receive about sex and romantic relationship. Ancient Eastern wisdom teaches that the essence of woman (or the feminine principle) is love. At his core, man (or the masculine principle) is pure awareness or presence. The conscious union of these two polarities is a tremendous force of power and good.

Rather than 'turning her on,' it is part of man's essential role as a lover to open a woman. Just as the warmth of the sun opens a flower to reveal its inner beauty, man is capable of awakening woman to her essential nature. She brings her loveliness; He brings his strength.

If man connects with woman in this way, it is love that he touches and brings to life. The act of making love has the power to bring a woman into a state of expansion and bliss, which translates into reverence of all life.

When a man consciously channels his vitality (male force) into his woman, she receives it and returns it to him, benefitting them both, and beyond. Being the recipient of her over-flowing love is <u>his</u> ultimate fulfilment. Quite literally, her pleasure is his pleasure. Then love-making becomes a prayer to life. As Diana Richardson[38] teaches,

---

[38] *Diana Richardson, teacher, and author of 'The Heart of Tantric Sex'*
(2003), 'Tantric Orgasm for Women' (2004), 'Tantric Sex for Men' (2009)

'Life changes its whole quality when the genitals are reserved to serve love.'

Different times and cultures have displayed greater or lesser degrees of ease and insight around physical intimacy and the potential divine nature of human sexuality. Tantra, the Tao, and other sacred teachings have revered the sexual arts as a pathway to bliss for centuries.

Many Eastern traditions teach that woman is God in female form, man in male form. When love-making becomes conscious, we see this divinity in our lover and want only to worship the beloved before us.

Osho,[39] the influential figure who made many ancient Eastern teachings accessible to the West, taught:

Love, but not as a need – as a sharing.
Love, but don't expect – give.
Love, but remember your love should not become an imprisonment for the other.
Love, but be very careful; you are moving on sacred ground.
You are going into the highest, the purest and holiest temple.
Be alert! Drop all impurities outside the temple.
When you love a person, love the person as if the person is a God, not less than that.
Never love a woman as a woman and never love a man as a man, because if you love a man as a man your love is going to be very, very ordinary.
If you love a woman as a woman, your love is not going to soar very high.
Love a woman as a goddess, then love becomes worship.

---

[39] *Osho (1931-1990), formerly known as Rajneesh, Indian mystic and new religious movement leader*

These are not empty words but a true expression of the awe and reverence which love-making can inspire. Find ways to honour the masculine, honour the feminine, as expressed in the form of the one(s) you share your heart, your bed and your life with.

Language reveals much about cultural attitudes. Comparing the origins of words for the sexual organs in English and Sanskrit, for example, demonstrates radically differing perspectives. The prosaic English term 'penis,' from Latin for 'tail,' contrasts with the Sanskrit 'lingam,' meaning 'wand of light.' The ancient Indian term expresses the nature of man's sexuality with his 'divine instrument' of love, healing and ecstasy.

Similarly, the Latin-derived 'vagina' gives us 'sheath' - reducing a woman's 'holiest of holies' to exist purely in relation to a man's penis. Sanskrit 'yoni,' on the other hand, translates as 'sacred space,' 'source of all life,' or 'gateway to the universe.' Within Hinduism, the yoni is honoured as the feminine generative power, emblem of the goddess Shakti. Her consort is the god, Shiva. He is worshipped as the male generative force of the world and honoured in a man's lingam and stylised phallic symbols.

How might our understanding of the gifts of sex be shaped if our language reflected a sacred reality? Likewise, if we were to frame intimate relationship and marriage as holy, where love and devotion preside, the ordinary would become the extraordinary.

Gabriel Horn gives a lovely, 'everyday' example from Native American traditions. 'There was a time when even to be allowed to brush the hair of their wives was an honour the women bestowed on their husbands, and that others could tell how loved a married woman was by the beauty of her hair. Men have mainly forgotten to braid the hair of

65

their wives, or decorate it with fine feathers or strips of pretty pelts.'[40]

In our own ways, in our own marriages, we each express the divine in human form, the spirit of life manifest in infinite ways.

[40] *Gabriel Horn - 'The Book of Ceremonies: A Native Way of Honouring and Living the Sacred' (2000)*

PART TWO

Creating Bespoke Wedding Ceremonies, Inspired by Folklore and Customs from Around the World

Introduction

The following chapters describe wedding traditions from different times and parts of the world. They are pooled from many sources, with gratitude to the global heritage now available to us. Where possible, I explore their background to give a greater appreciation of them.

Many of these traditions are ancient. Some are versions of older customs, adapted to meet changing times. The meaning of a particular custom may have been lost or distorted, and sometimes research offers contradictory origins or interpretations. Other ideas included here are new altogether, created in response to an individual or collective need to express something in a certain way.

This reminds us that, to fulfil its purpose, any form of ritual or ceremony needs to be alive. To be alive, there must be a reason and a felt connection behind each element included in a rite. This allows for change and adaptation to suit the *actual* situation or people involved.

We also remember that ritual is powerful because it speaks the language of myth, symbols, images and archetypes. This engages the deepest parts of ourselves, well below our rational minds, initiating transformation at a cellular level. It nourishes our spirit.

Whether folk, religious, secular, or contemporary, the customs here are offered as inspiration to create personally-meaningful wedding ceremonies. The idea is to encourage reflection and personal expression, so please use any that speak to you.

You might want to hold this sort of question close: What moves or touches you? An idea or custom in its entirety, or the essence *behind* it which you can then give your own form to? What do you want your marriage to be grounded in? What ritual, symbols, or ongoing commitment practices most inspire, support and reflect these values?

Be bold, be creative. Listen to yourself and absorb or adapt the traditions that feel relevant or hint at the inner transformation you seek.

The Nature of Weddings

In many cultures, weddings have been celebrated *over several days*. We need time to transition from one state of being to another. Marking the initial crossing the threshold with due reverence and celebration is a major help in beginning to 'register' the transition or change of status taking place.

When exploring the wedding customs which follow, let's remember that many of them may have been part of several days of preparation and celebration. There can be 'rituals within rituals.'

Weddings have typically been lengthy and inclusive, whole community affairs. Western culture has often lost sight of this. The fact that today we are more likely to spend a mere few hours celebrating a wedding changes things.

Nowadays, it's also common to be invited only to the 'party after.' This means some guests do not attend the ceremony, denying an experience of shared participation. Similarly, when children are explicitly excluded from such important events, everyone is deprived of essential life-affirming experiences. George Monbiot[41] says that 'A community not built around children is no community at all.'

[41] *George Monbiot (b. 1963) - British author, environmental & political activist, from a Guardian article 'The Child Inside,' 7th January 2015*

CHAPTER SEVEN

Beginning to Plan and Structure a Wedding Ceremony

Ritual is a journey consisting of three basic processes: Preparation, Manifestation and Closure. Each element is included for a reason, and each is part of the whole, held within the powerful container of transformative space.

The heart of a wedding ceremony is the declaration of two lives joining. Everything that precedes and follows *supports* this 'crossing-the-threshold' moment. Bearing this in mind may help you know what to include.

Some elements of a ritual are important for setting the scene. They help people feel welcome, safe and clear about the purpose of the occasion. Anything that unifies the group in shared purpose is good.

Some practices are designed to build energy and raise power to facilitate the desired change of consciousness. Communal singing, dancing and drumming are prime examples of this.

When the 'work' is done, the threshold crossed, everyone must be transitioned back out of the ceremonial space, so there will also be elements that support this in a wedding ceremony.

1. **Preparation** - clarifying purpose and then preparing accordingly

The more focused the intention behind a ritual, the more powerful it is. Once you are clear on your purpose, you can make wise choices about the flow and content of the ceremony to best express that.

2. **Manifestation** - the wedding ceremony itself

The ritual begins by preparing sacred space. This can be established physically and energetically by defining, clearing, decorating and dedicating it to serve the purpose of the ritual.

God/Spirit/Life can be invoked to guide and hold the proceedings. Older cultures called on the ancestors and the spirit and natural worlds to 'please come and be with us in such a way that we can feel you and fulfil the purpose of this ritual.'[42]

Remember how important the presence of your loved ones is. Marianne Williamson[43] writes that their 'collective prayers form a circle of light and protection around the relationship.'

3. **Closure** - ending a ceremony well, facilitating 'the return'

All that was opened at the beginning must be closed. Anything invoked needs releasing and thanking. Energetic closure and a deliberate exiting of ritual space are important, along with physically clearing it.

---

[42] *Sobonfu Somé - 'The Spirit of Intimacy: Ancient Teachings in the Ways of Relationships' (1997)*

[43] *Marianne Williamson (b. 1952) - American author, spiritual teacher & activist*

Expressing gratitude is an effective way of ending, acknowledging the two-way energetic exchange that has just taken place.

Making merry routinely marks the end of any rite. As well as serving an important social role, festive eating, drinking and dancing help 'ground' all who have participated in the non-ordinary realms of ceremony. It also sets the marriage off on a footing of abundance and joy.

The Role of Celebrant

Historically, and sometimes still today, the religious or 'official' leader of a community automatically performs the wedding rite. However, those couples seeking guidance, exploration and a ceremony to reflect them personally may want to choose who they entrust with this role carefully.

A good celebrant-minister (of any religion or none) can be a font of knowledge, wisdom and creativity around the practicalities, content and crafting of a wedding ceremony. Their role can extend far beyond the tangible. They are there to hold the safe container within which sacred process takes place.

Celebrant and couple form a working partnership. The couple need to ask, or *call forth,* whatever they innately know they need in order to *feel* initiated.

On the other hand, the celebrant must call forth their own strengths of presence, integrity and connection. They are the *conduit* through which the power and grace of initiation flow.

Ask this of your chosen celebrant, and let them ask of you. You, along with your community of family and friends, are in something together. And that 'something' delivers to you as much as you can ask of it.

And Finally...

THERE ARE NO RIGHTS OR WRONGS in what you choose to include in your wedding ceremony and how you put it together. If it works for you, that is what matters.

For some people, following familiar patterns lends a ritual gravitas precisely *because* they are traditional. For others, 'personalising' each element is what makes their ceremony meaningful.

A ceremony may be fully 'scripted' in advance, or there may be a mix of structure to hand with room for spontaneity. Non-prepared words or gestures that 'come through' in ritual often speak more directly than anything prepared. Grace has exquisite, sometimes uncanny, ways of communicating if we allow it.

Powerful rites of passage can happen with no pre-arranged structure in place at all. People gather in sacred space, set an intention and then open themselves so that life can fulfil the purpose of the ceremony. It is wonderful to speak *directly* with Source.

We may not be confident yet to commune so directly and freely in this way. We may need the safety and rhythm that structure or familiarity can provide. In contemporary Western culture at least, there tends to be a rough formula that wedding ceremonies follow.

To be as user-friendly as possible, what follows in the next few chapters is a guide to possible elements for inclusion in a wedding ceremony. I describe various ways of expressing different components, drawing on the history, inspiration and traditions of many countries.

I invite you to 'mix and match' them in any way that suits, adapting where necessary, or placing elements in the order that best serves.

I reiterate: There is no definitive way of doing any of this; whatever makes your heart sing is the way to go!

CHAPTER EIGHT

Preparatory Rituals and Customs

The change in status from single to married generally marked a much greater life transition in the past than today. To varying degrees, marriage has signified a transition from youth to adulthood, sexual awakening and starting a home and family.

In addition, for women, it has often meant marrying into her husband's family while being uprooted from her own. Furthermore, before reliable contraception, women were often expected to give up their paid work the day before their wedding. From then on, their world was dominated by housework and caring for their husband and children.

This section explores some of the many rituals which acknowledge the impact of these significant life changes. These are typically less defined or immense nowadays if both partners earn a living, live together, or even start a family before marriage.

They take place *before* the wedding day itself, in the time of 'engagement' or, more archaically, 'betrothal,' Much care and attention are given to getting everything 'just right.'

It can feel as if this sets the tone for the marriage to come.

A wedding and its preparations have often included a whole community. The occasion brings fun and colour to hard-working lives. The women often celebrate with the bride-to-be, while the groom celebrates with the men.

Proposal and Betrothal/Engagement Customs

There were many old rites associated with securing an agreement to marry, either amongst a couple themselves and/or via their parents on their behalf. Here are just a few examples:

♡ In her book on Scottish customs,[44] Bennett describes a very old practice from Orkney where young couples entered sacredly-binding engagements by visiting two temples together. At the Temple of the Moon, witnessed by the man, the woman prayed for a blessed marriage. Next, the man prayed similarly in the Temple of the Sun. Lastly, they went to the 'Stone of Odin.' Joining hands through the hole in the stone, they made their vows.

♡ Bennett also described the old ritual of the 'contract' or 'arrangement' that took place at the bride's house and was as special as the wedding itself. It was a playful evening of wit and merry-making, where the bride's father was asked for his consent, although the marriage had already been approved. The groom and his friends 'bartered' for the bride, beginning by referring to a household object (eg. 'I believe you have a very precious jug') and finally naming the 'precious daughter.'

---

[44] *Margaret Bennett - 'Scottish Customs: from the Cradle to the Grave'* *(1992)*

In Roman times, a betrothed young woman was given the dress of a wife. Her girlish clothing was offered to the household gods, and then she was removed from her playmates and trained into the duties of a wife.

♡ Old lore of the British Isles allowed a woman to propose every leap year, on February 29th. Any man rejecting her offer had to pay a fine, ranging from a kiss to money, a dress or gloves.

Dowry or Bride Price

Many cultures have included the exchange of money or other valuable commodities (eg. land, property, or cattle) when negotiating a marriage contract. In some cultures, where a family loses the valued labour of a daughter, the suitor pays a 'bride price' in compensation. In other times and places where the husband supports his wife, the bride's family pay a dowry to him.

Women prepared items for their all-important 'marriage-chest' or 'dowry box' from an early age. They were variously known as the 'bride-wain' (medieval Britain), 'glory box' (Australia and New Zealand), 'hope box' (US), 'bottom drawer' (UK). This prized box typically contained embroidered clothes and sheets, plus other household items, which were made and gathered with pride.

♡ Medieval Britain - girls often included lucky lace-making bobbins carved from the bones of wedding feasts they had attended.

♡ Germany - long ago, trees were planted at the birth of a girl. Once engaged, the trees were cut down to pay for her dowry.

Invitation to the Wedding

♡ Germany - in old Bavarian tradition, an official 'Inviter' issued a wedding invitation to each household in the form of a personal rhyme. Adorned with ribbons and flowers, an invitation was accepted by taking one of his ribbons and pinning it to his hat.

The Best Man and Bridesmaids

Today, both the bride and groom typically have a carefully chosen friend, or friends, who play a significant role throughout the wedding preparations and on the day itself. There tends to be a designated 'chief bridesmaid' or 'matron of honour' and main 'best man.'

One of their many roles is to organise the stag or hen do (see below). The 'best man's speech' has also long been an integral part of wedding revelries. This is becoming more expected of the chief bridesmaid too nowadays.

Originally, the 'best man' was chosen for his fighting skills rather than his close connection with the groom. There have been times when women were forced into marriage, so the main role of the original 'best man' was to prevent her escape! He might have even kidnapped the bride in the first place and had to be prepared to fend off attacks during the wedding. For a similar reason, the bride stood to the left of her groom (still the tradition today) so that his sword arm was free.

The origin of bridesmaids and ushers perhaps comes from ancient Roman law that required ten witnesses at a wedding. They all dressed the same as the bride or groom to confuse any ill-wishing spirits who would not know which was the wedding couple.

Stag and Hen Parties

Hen and Stag parties have become a rite of passage almost intrinsic to today's Western wedding celebrations. The origins of these single-sex gatherings go back at least as far as ancient Greece, and it is interesting to track their rise and fall over the ages.

Stag Dos

Male pre-wedding celebrations are thought to have originated within the military 2,500 years ago in Greece. The night before a wedding, a groom-to-be was celebrated with raucous feasting, toasting the end of his youth, life ahead, and continued loyalty to his comrades.

Stag or bachelor parties typically involve drinking, pranks and humiliation of the groom. In the UK, they increased in popularity from the 1980s when pub crawls became the norm. From the 1990s, strippers often featured, and sometime later, weekend breaks.

Hen Nights/Parties/Dos

Evidence for these rites dates back nearly 4,000 years to Greece. There was a specific pre-marriage ritual called 'Proaulia,' marking the transition from girl to woman. Offerings of old toys, clothes and a lock of hair were made to Artemis, the special protector of young girls and goddess of virginity and childbirth. The blessings of Aphrodite, Hera, or Athena were also invoked.

The original term 'hen party' referred to any gathering of women. It became the name of all-female bridal celebrations in the UK around the 1960s. Before this, there were many workplace rituals that marked the end of a woman's paid working life and her entry into domesticity and motherhood.

These had regional names such as 'ribbon girl,' 'pay off,' 'taking out,' 'jumping the chanty,' and the 'bride's ritual' and took place in factories and offices for at least a century. Women were typically dressed as mock brides and paraded around while colleagues both congratulated and teased them.

Parties gradually moved away from the workplace to a pub or club. By the 1980s, it was barely more than a night out with a few women friends. The original purpose - celebrating a woman's 'Last Night of Freedom' - had largely disappeared.

The tradition had a huge resurgence in the 1990s, with fancy dress, limousines, sports activities, drinking and dancing. As with the stags, strippers became increasingly popular.

A decade later, the hen 'night' began to turn into 'weekend breaks' and holidays abroad. The 'bride-to-be' sash and mock veil are still essential accessories, but the emphasis now is on spending time together and having fun.

Other Countries

♡ Sweden - friends would often spend a celebratory evening in the bathhouse with the bride or groom.

♡ US - 'Bridal' or 'Wedding Showers' are gift-giving parties for the bride or couple respectively. This is typically a daytime, women-only event where the bride is 'showered' with the necessary goods and finances to enable the wedding to take place.

♡ Brazil - the equivalent of the bridal shower here is called the 'kitchen shower,' as gifts are more explicitly related to the setting up of a new home.

Fun, Games and Gifts

Wedding preparations the world over tend to express a great out-pouring of the wider community's care and support of a couple. In addition to joyous celebration, practical considerations are also included, such as keeping harm at bay, invoking fertility, or helping financially.

♡ *Krevati* (Greece) - this old custom (meaning 'bed') took place in the couple's new home. Before partying together, family and friends put money and young children on the couple's bed for prosperity and fertility.

♡ *Polterabend* (Germany) - this informal 'evening of making a racket' takes place the night before the wedding. China and porcelain are smashed for good luck - an example of the widely-held superstitions surrounding brides and malignant spirits where noise is made to scare them away.

A contemporary interpretation suggests that while crockery may break, the marriage never will. The couple clear up the broken pieces to end the ritual, representing the teamwork needed to sustain their marriage.

♡ Feet-Washing (Scotland) - the riotous custom of washing the couple's feet happened the night before the wedding itself. The foot-washing was constantly alternated with 'blackening' - originally with soot (and later with shoe polish, cocoa, chocolate or treacle etc.), which started with the feet but, inevitably, ended up everywhere.

'Blackenings' of the groom were much rougher. He could be 'tarred and feathered,' clothed or unclothed, with anything sticky. Sometimes he was held upside down to mark the ceiling with his feet.

♡ Finland - a bride-to-be traditionally went around her community collecting wedding gifts in a pillowcase. She was often accompanied by an older, married man holding an umbrella over her head, symbolising protection.

♡ 'Give-Away' (First Nations America) - instead of receiving gifts, the couple gave away many of their possessions in gratitude to those who had cared for them.

♡ 'Rubbing Shoulders' (Scotland) - between the reading of the banns and the wedding day itself, young unmarried friends would rub shoulders with the couple, hoping for similar luck.

Ritual Cleansing

Ritual bathing followed by anointing with relevant oils dates back thousands of years.

Water renews us for a clean, fresh beginning. Essential oils add a sense of sacredness and are often chosen for the meanings attributed to them.

Some cultures place great emphasis on the bride being completely devoid of body hair for her wedding day. Women's hands are painted with intricate henna designs in many Arab, Asian and African cultures.

The Morning of the Wedding

Often the bride and groom are separated the night before the wedding, not meeting until the ceremony itself.

♡ Southern Germany/Austria - a bride was greeted at dawn by the sound of gunshot or fire-crackers.

♡ Scotland - while the women breakfasted together, two men arrived to demand the bride. After mock resistance, they eventually broke in and escorted her to the church. She led the way, never looking back.

Old shoes, brooms and scrubbing brushes were thrown after the bride and groom as they left their respective homes. Pipers and gunshots accompanied the two processions. Each group carried whisky, bread and cheese to offer the first person they met en route.

♡ Shetland Isles (Scotland) - the groom and his friends lined up in front of the bride's house. A gun was fired, but only after the third shot did the bride appear, leading her women in such a way that each man got to kiss each woman.

Wedding Attire

The Dress

The white wedding dress is relatively recent, popularised by Queen Victoria at her own wedding in 1840. At this time, it represented wealth, as white was both expensive to buy and difficult to keep clean. Later Victorian values associated it with purity, chastity and innocence.

For most of European history, brides simply wore their best dress. That said, it does seem there have been preferred colours at different times and places:

Blue - symbolised purity, perhaps because of its associations with the Virgin Mary. In ancient Israel, the bride's dress included a blue border, and Irish women occasionally wear a blue wedding dress to this day.

Red - China, India, and other Eastern cultures have long held red as their traditional wedding colour. It signifies love, joy and prosperity. In many parts of Asia, unmarried women are not permitted to wear red. Early Celts also favoured red, the colour of fertility. It remained the most popular colour in Britain up until the mid-1800s.

Black - if marrying a widower or was herself widowed, a bride typically wore black.

White - represented joy to the ancient Greeks, and sometimes they painted their bodies white before getting married.

Green - signified both good or bad fortune, depending on the culture. Green is the colour of Venus, the Roman Goddess of love, and still popular in Italian weddings today.

The unlucky connotations of green come from its association with nature and the fairy folk.

To wear it might invite the 'little people' to cause harm.

♡   This rhyme dates back to the mid-1800s:

> *Married in White, you have chosen right*
> *Married in Grey, you will go far away*
> *Married in Black, you will wish yourself back,*
> *Married in Red, you will wish yourself dead,*
> *Married in Green, ashamed to be seen,*
> *Married in Blue, you will always be true,*

Married in Pearl, you will live in a whirl,
Married in Yellow, ashamed of your fellow,
Married in Brown, you will live in the town,
Married in Pink, your spirits will sink.

♡ It was bad luck to try on a completed dress before the wedding day, so a small section of the hem was left unfinished until the last minute.

♡ This old rhyme reminds the bride of what she must include in her wedding attire to ensure maximum good fortune:

Something old, something new,
Something borrowed, something blue
'And a lucky sixpence in her shoe'

Wearing 'something old' - connects the bride to her past, a sense of familiarity.

'Something new' – signifies a new chapter.

'Something borrowed' - an item was borrowed from a happily married woman so that her happiness is transferred to the new bride.

'Something blue' – often a blue or blue-trimmed garter today, blue represents loyalty, also purity. Old associations link it to the heavens and the divine.

And a lucky sixpence in her shoe' - this last line is often forgotten today, but a coin in the shoe once invoked prosperity.

Shoes

Shoes and good fortune seem to be closely associated in many cultures:

♡ Germany - Mothers put dill and other lucky herbs into their daughter's right wedding shoe.

♡ Sweden - the bride's mother gave her a gold coin for her right shoe and her father a silver coin for her left

♡ Scotland - the bride must put on her right shoe first and carry a silver coin in her stocking (or pocket).

♡ Poland - a bride must not wear open-toed footwear, lest the good fortune be lost.

The Veil

This custom probably pre-dates Greek and Roman times. It has been attributed different meanings, ranging from protecting the bride from evil, to symbolising her purity and virginity, to deceiving the groom (eg. in arranged marriages).

Wearing the veil of a happily married woman is considered lucky. Nowadays, the old custom can lend a sense of mystery while representing crossing a threshold.

Other Attire and Bridal Accessories

♡ China - a red parasol signified luck and protection.

♡ Germany - brides carried a pearl, representing the moon and the goddess Diana.

♡ Scottish Isles - daughters were given amber necklaces the night before their wedding as a talisman and heirloom.

♡ Sudan - the groom gives his bride a red and gold shawl to wear for the wedding.

♡ Horseshoes - brides often carry a 'Lucky Horseshoe', kept upright to prevent any good fortune from falling out. Horseshoes have been associated with supernatural powers since pre-Christian times. Shaped like a crescent moon, the Greeks saw them as a fertility symbol.

♡ Silver Sixpence - first minted in England in 1551, it became associated with weddings almost immediately. Brides were often given a sixpence by the lord of the manor and, in later times, by her parents. It came to represent luck, even until today.

Timing of Weddings

Many cultures place the utmost importance on determining the most auspicious time for a wedding. Astrology and birth charts are taken seriously. Practical reasons generally dictate the timing in the West. Sometimes an anniversary, or another significant date, is chosen.

You may like to consider the significance of the season, time of day, or moon phase when deciding your wedding date. There is much old country lore (some of it contradictory!) around all of this.

♡ The following attributes refer to the day that a proposal of marriage is made:

Monday - means the couple will lead eventful lives
Tuesday - for harmony
Wednesday - a life without quarrels
Thursday - each will achieve their goals
Friday - hard work to be successful
Saturday - for a compatible, pleasurable life

Sunday - no proposal should be made on 'the Lord's Day'

♡ This old rhyme refers to the wedding day itself:

> *Monday for health*
> *Tuesday for wealth*
> *Wednesday best of all*
> *Thursday for losses*
> *Friday for crosses,*
> *Saturday for no luck at all.*

♡ In some traditions, Friday was the favoured wedding day as it is named after the Norse Goddess Freya. The Roman counterpart was Venus, whose day was also Friday (reflected in the French *Vendredi)*. Both Goddesses bestow love and joy and are associated with sexuality, fertility and femininity.

♡ Traditionally, ministers would not perform weddings during Lent, which ruled out most of February to April.

♡ May - For Celtic-influenced cultures, May was a blessed and joyous time. Known as the 'Merry Month', life, sexuality and pleasure were celebrated, reflecting the greening of the land. Ritual promiscuity in this season was wide-spread in Europe until more puritan attitudes developed from the seventeenth century.

♡ June - always the lucky, 'marrying month,' June is named after Juno, goddess of marriage, birth, love and happiness.

♡ Winter Weddings - in ancient Greece most weddings took place during the 'Union-Month' of *Gamelion* (the equivalent of January). This was associated with Hera, the goddess of hearth, home and marriage.

♡ Winter Solstice - there is beautiful symbolism in a midwinter wedding where the longest night gives way to the returning light and life begins anew.

♡ Leap Year - in Anglo-Saxon times, it was fortuitous to marry in a leap year.

♡ Poland - any month containing the letter 'r' is deemed lucky. In Polish, this means that March, June, August, September, October and December are ideal.

♡ Morning energy brings freshness, brightness, and a sense of promise. At noon, the sun is at the peak of its energy, the highest it will climb in the sky. Some traditions (eg. Zoroastrianism) favour dusk as the time for weddings. Day merging into night symbolises two lives joining.

♡ Some cultures - including Chinese and Victorian England - believed it lucky to marry on the half-hour rather than the hour. The hands of the clock then travel upwards, symbolising an increase in good fortune.

Phases of the Moon

Waxing Moon - the energy at this time is of growth and gathering power, so it is supportive of new beginnings.

Waning Moon - the moon's strength and light decrease in this fortnight. The focus turns inwards.

Full Moon - for three days, the moon is at the height of her brightness and power - this is a lovely energy to have reflected in your marriage.

♡ Shetland Isles (Scotland) - weddings traditionally took place at a new moon for luck.

Reflective Ideas for the Period of Engagement

Most traditions leading up to the main wedding rite are externally-focused, often communal and flamboyant. Yet the engagement period also invites inner reflection and quieter, more intimate ways of connecting with the momentous process that 'getting married' can be.

The more this process is engaged with, the deeper and more fulfilling the experience is likely to be. It is an invaluable opportunity to focus internally, to reflect on our heart's longings and our blocks to love. Much soul's growth can happen.

Anything that brings us closer to ourselves is helpful. There is no formula but an invitation to follow the impulse of your heart. It might be to journal, meditate, sing, dance, pray, or paint. Perhaps you create a sacred space in which to hone your intentions, do some internal 'tidying,' ask for guidance, or rest in Grace.

I share a few suggestions below.

Inner Work and Healing

The inner journey will, of course, be different for everyone. We each carry wounds, vulnerabilities and unresolved relationship challenges. Many of these can be healed *through* an intimate relationship, deep inquiry and/or skilled professional input.

Many speak of the 'inner marriage' – the uniting of all aspects of ourselves into one integrated whole. In essence, the more we can love and accept ourselves, the greater our capacity to give and receive love from another.

The inner 'tidying' could include an 'inventory' of previous romantic relationships. Sobonfu Somé,[45] for example, worked extensively with couples *prior* to their marriage. One of the healing rituals she offered included the energetic release of any unhelpful ties or residual pain from past relationships in order to move forward freely.

Mindful Hen and Stag Parties

There is something archetypal and beautiful about women celebrating together and men celebrating together before woman and man unite in marriage.

Even the concept of a 'Sacred Stag' or 'Holy Hen' party could add fresh awareness and inspiration to these events. Whichever creative form this takes needs to be authentic to all present.

Spending Time in Reflection

These questions[46] offer couples a framework to explore their relationship, name what is important to them, and help identify the vision for their marriage.

1. Where, when and how did you first meet - what is your 'story' together?

2. What attracted you to each other when you first met?

3. How did your relationship develop and strengthen into what it is today?

---

[45] *Sobonfu Somé (d. 2017) - of the Dagara people of Burkina Faso, Somé brought her West African heritage and teachings to the West.*
[46] *Most of these are from my Interfaith training (2002-2004) with Miranda Holden.*

4. What is the most important aspect of your relationship to each of you?

5. What is it that you really love and appreciate about the other?

6. What is your vision for the future together?

7. Why marriage? Why now?

8. What gifts are you bringing to one another and the marriage?

9. What do you see as the highest purpose of your relationship?

10. What are your areas of strength as a couple?

11. Where would you like to become stronger? How?

12. Do you have any expectations/conditions/assumptions for being together (eg. Fidelity? Honesty? Around jobs, money, children?)

13. Are there any particular challenges or issues surrounding getting married?

14. What do you wish your marriage ceremony to accomplish?

15. Do you have any spiritual/religious, moral or philosophical worldviews that you would like reflected in the ceremony?

16. Are there any words or symbols you would prefer not to have in your ceremony?

CHAPTER NINE

The Central Wedding Ceremony

An Example Outline of a Wedding Ceremony

This chapter explores possible elements to include in a wedding ceremony, leaving full scope for personal taste and creativity. Prayers, readings, songs and blessings can be interspersed throughout.

- ♥ Procession/Entrance
- ♥ Opening Words/Welcome, including 'Attunement'
- ♥ Invocation
- ♥ Guest Declaration(s)
- ♥ Honouring of Family Members
- ♥ Ritual Element
- ♥ Address
- ♥ Vows
- ♥ Blessing and Exchange of Rings
- ♥ Pronouncement
- ♥ Kiss
- ♥ Affirmation of Community
- ♥ Closure
- ♥ Exit

Setting Up/Arranging the Space

This includes anything that prepares the physical space in advance of the ritual.

Couples often take great care in selecting both the location and the aesthetics of their ceremonial space. The look and feel of a place can be very important in creating a sense of welcome and sacredness. Sometimes there is a particular theme.

It is valuable to carefully consider the 'container' in which the rite of passage takes place. This could be a room itself or a space created using rocks, flowers, shells, coloured scarves, or a grove of trees, for example. Guests in an inclusive horse-shoe or circle arrangement add to the sense of 'holding' the space and the couple.

♡ Flowing Water - in some cultures, water plays an essential role. Indonesian weddings were traditionally held near rivers, streams or fountains, representing the ever-flowing nature of love.

♡ Facing East: In some traditions (eg. the Navajos of indigenous America), the couple face East - the direction of the rising sun and therefore symbolic of a new life.

♡ Altar - a table, shrine or altar creates a natural focus, a place of beauty and power at the heart of a ceremony. Any personally meaningful or supportive object has a place on your wedding altar. These can represent things or people you love, qualities you would like to manifest in your marriage, and any guidance you call upon.

♡ Cleansing or Blessing the Space

- 'Smudging' - a purifying technique of many cultures, where the smoke of incense or herbs is used to consecrate space.

- Sound - in the form of a rattle(s), bell, drum or voice - is another way of energising a space. It 'cuts through' what has been before, leaving a space zinging and ringing.

- Sweeping - a broom sweeps away anything from the past that no longer serves to make way for the new.

♥ Procession/Entrance

The ceremony itself can only begin once the bride and groom are present. There are many different ways in which they can arrive, separately or together.

♡ In many cultures, the bride and groom are accompanied by their female and male friends respectively.

Eg. on the island of Anjouan, off the East African coast, drummers lead in the groom.

Eg. in Afghanistan, the bride enters like a queen, with her entourage of regally-dressed women and sometimes young children.

♡ The bride and/or groom may already be seated on throne-like chairs as guests enter.

♡ In the West, the groom waits at the altar as the bride processes in.

♡ The bride and groom may enter together, alone or supported by a chosen few.

Eg. In Sweden, couples traditionally walked down the aisle together.

Eg. In Poland, the couple entered together, followed by their parents and two witnesses.

♡ In British tradition, the bride is accompanied by her father down the aisle. Jewish custom has the bride flanked by both parents.

♡ Call and Response - The most stirring wedding entrance I ever witnessed evoked a sense of answering the call of another's heart. The groom beat a drum on the shore of a Norwegian fjord. His bride, from a boat, answered in her own rhythm. Groom called again, bride responded, until their drum beats got closer and closer.

♡ Door/Arch - this signifies entering sacred space and crossing a threshold.

♡ In Denmark, the couple enter through the 'gate of honour,' traditionally made of pine, beech or oak branches.

♡ Aisle/Procession

'The walk' that often marks the formal beginning of a wedding rite can symbolise treading life's path. This 'walk of a life-time'[47] deserves savouring, with each step and breath carrying us consciously towards the new.

♡ Accompanying the Bride down the Aisle

---

[47] *Susannah Stefanachi Macomb with Andrea Thompson - 'Joining Hands and Hearts: Interfaith, Intercultural Wedding Celebrations' (2003)*

I find the tradition of a bride being 'given away' by her father or father-figure challenging. Perhaps it expresses something of the sacred dance between masculine and feminine, lost in our times.

I offer a re-framing of 'walking down the aisle' devoid of authoritarian connotations. These examples honour close kinship at a key life event:

The celebrant asks the father who has accompanied his daughter down the aisle:

Who supports __ in her marriage to __? - I do.

This beautiful bride was accompanied to her groom by her father. Have you done so in confidence of the love and welcome that she will receive? - I have.

Thank you, to you and to _____ (bride's mother) for giving life to this woman who stands here today.

Celebrant to both sets of parents:

Who has guided these people through life, nurtured and loved them, encouraged their independence? (Parents stand)
Who supports them as they join in marriage? - We do

♡ Bridal Party

A bride's entourage often includes her father, a few female friends, and children in the role of flower girls or pageboys.

♡ In some traditions, the 'matron of honour' must be a happily married woman to bestow her good fortune to the marriage taking place.

♡ Latvia - bride and groom choose a favourite married couple to support them at their wedding, rather than a best man or chief bridesmaid.

♡ Shetland Isles - a married couple called the 'honest folk' led the procession and hosted the celebrations.

♡ Flower girls originally scattered petals before the bride, marking out a path of happiness and beauty.

♡ The Bouquet - perhaps originated as a protective charm, rather than a pretty posy. The bridal bouquets of ancient Greece were made of particular herbs and spices.

♡ Japan - live pairs of cranes or geese were sometimes part of the bridal procession as they mate for life.

♥ Welcome

Opening words are needed to help people feel at ease. The intention of the ritual can be clearly named.

Offering a simple practice of 'Attunement,' such as music, a communal greeting, a reminder to notice body and breath, or feel their feet on the ground, can support guests to be as present as possible. It can be helpful to remind all present that they are likely united by a shared love of the bride and/or groom and a wish for their happiness.

♡ Passing the Sign of Peace - The interfaith minister Susanna Macomb often incorporates this Christian tradition at the beginning of weddings to bring people together:

In the spirit of love and unity, the bride and groom have asked that we pass the sign of peace. For those...not familiar with this ritual, simply offer a handshake to your neighbours, with the words 'Peace be with you.' If you feel so inspired, a hug or a kiss would be most appropriate as well![48]

♥ Invocation

This is an opportunity to bring in anything that helps shift the focus from the secular to the sacred. It calls forth larger energies to bless and guide the ritual and its effect.

♥ Guest Declaration(s)

As the celebrant, I often include a 'guest declaration(s)' early in a ceremony to help people feel included. Essentially, all present are asked to affirm their intention to support their friends in marriage.

Eg. *If you pledge to support _____ & _____ through whatever lies ahead for them, would you please stand now and say, 'We do'? Guests: We do!*

This also offers another opportunity to be creative, get personal, and really hone in on what matters to you. I encourage you to reflect on your friendships, values, and journey together as you talk through the unique kind of things you would want **your** friends and family to do to support **you**.

Friends of mine, for example, asked these deeply considered questions of their guests:

1. *Will you seek us out, wherever we are, for chats, fun weekends and cups of tea? - We will!*

---

[48] *Susannah Stefanachi Macomb with Andrea Thompson - 'Joining Hands and Hearts: Interfaith, Intercultural Wedding Celebrations' (2003)*

2. *If you have a stronger relationship with one of us, will you find ways to know the other better?*

3. *Will you ask us how our relationship is and encourage us to be honest?*

4. *When we over-think things or get too anxious or serious, will you help us to laugh at ourselves?*

5. *When our love for each other needs nurturing or repairing, will you listen well, take both our sides and remind us of what we have said today?*

6. *Will you share your own struggles and celebrations in love and life so we can put ours in context and so we can return your friendship?*

7. *Will you dance, eat, drink and be merry with us tonight and in the years to come?*[49]

♥ Honouring of Family Members

A wedding offers a rare opportunity to publicly express gratitude and acknowledge close family ties. We can honour the fundamental role of our primary caregivers and receive their support and blessing.

Gratitude to the Parents

♡ Tibet - a 'breast price' was paid to the bride's family in gratitude to the mother for nurturing the bride as an infant.

---

[49] *Simon & Maro, used with their kind permission, from their 'Non-Wedding Wedding' in 2012*

♡ Sudan - the couple kiss the knees of their parents, seeking their blessing and expressing continued devotion.

♡ A representative from each of the couple's families can light a candle in recognition of the two family lines.

Blessings from the Parents

♡ In some cultures, there is allocated space within a wedding ceremony for both sets of parents to bless the couple formally.

♡ Indonesia - traditionally, the bride's mother placed a flower garland around the groom's neck. Nowadays, each mother presents her future son/daughter-in-law with a garland.

Acknowledging Deceased Loved Ones

Here are some personal examples which acknowledge a precious absence without it becoming too heavy.

1. Where the groom's mother has died: *'We acknowledge that her spirit resides among us today. ___ says he can feel her smiling down on him today. She remains and will always remain in ___'s and his father's hearts. The lilies here today are dedicated to her.*[50]

2. Where the bride's father has died: *'___ misses her father ___ very much and says she knows he surely would not have missed this event. He so often wondered who she would marry, and is probably quite*

---

[50] *I was inspired by these words years ago but failed to note the author and title of this book. My humble apologies and gratitude to the author.*

surprised that _____ is not a musician, artist or poet....'51

Acknowledging a Wedding Couple's Own Children

It is important to include any children in their parent's wedding. They can be given a specific role, eg. bearing the rings or being invited to blow bubbles or throw petals over their parents.

Words can be used which simply name how it is:

1. *This ceremony today not only celebrates ___ & ___'s love and union as a couple but also their love as a family. Their beloved son, ___, is a precious part of their journey together so far.*

2. Speaking to the couple with their child(ren):

   Blessings on you all three as a family and to any other children who may come to join you. May love and understanding reside in your home and your hearts.

Including Children from Previous Relationships

The impact of a parent (re-)marrying can be enormous on a child and generally requires careful handling by all the adults involved. Reassuring a child that they will always be loved and their thoughts and feelings taken into account set good foundations for the new family constellation that is emerging.

---

[51] *Same book as above*

These are personal examples from a book[52] where the celebrant spoke directly to the child(ren) before the vow-taking:

1. Where the bride already has two children: ___ & ___, *your mum and ___ want you to know just how important you both are and that you will always be in their lives. They love you very much and want your blessing. Will you join me in blessing their marriage?'* All put their hands on the couple's hands, close their eyes, and take a silent moment together.

2. In another scenario, the celebrant addressed the groom's adolescent children personally. She drew on their father's own words, who had replied 'my kids' when asked about his top priority in life. He also described being reunited with them, after a long custody battle, as the happiest day of his life.

3. Where the groom has two daughters: ___ & ___, *your dad calls you his incredible, amazing girls. He says he loves your happy dancing feet. You have taught him so many things… ___ and your dad want you to know how very much they love you, and how important you are and always will be in their lives.*

♥ Ritual Elements

Offering Food and Drink

In many traditions, the couple symbolically offer each other food or drink. This simple act of sharing represents life and

---

[52] *I was inspired by these words years ago but failed to note the author and title of this book. My humble apologies and gratitude to the author.*

sustenance. The gesture may represent a couple's intention to look after each other, share all that they have and nourish their marriage always.

♡   Lithuania - couples are given wine (happiness), salt (tears), and then bread (work) in recognition of the nature of marriage.

♡   Russia - bread and salt symbolise hospitality. During the ceremony, they are given to the couple to represent health, prosperity and longevity. At the reception, they are a sign of welcome by the groom's parents.

♡   Navajo, a First Nation's people - the couple share white and yellow maize, representing the masculine and the feminine.

♡   Greece - the couple eat honey and walnuts from silver spoons. Walnuts are made up of four parts, representing the union of the couple and their two families.

♡   Indonesia - the couple share turmeric rice three times. Rice represents abundance and fertility and turmeric, eternal love.

♡   Africa - In some parts, the ingredients used in this tradition each represents an aspect of life, ending with the sweetness of honey:

Lemon juice - sorrow
Vinegar - bitterness
Cayenne pepper - passion
Kola nuts - strength
Palm oil - peace and serenity
Water - purification and blessing
Honey - sweetness

♡ Breaking and sharing of bread between the couple and guests is an ancient wedding tradition.

In parts of Eastern Europe, the mothers present the couple with a loaf of bread which they tear apart and eat.

♡ Morocco - the couple drink milk together and share a date, symbolising life's sweet nourishment.

♡ A Contemporary 'Feeding Ritual' by Robert Fulghum.[53]

Here is an excerpt from one of the weddings he conducted:

To the wedding guests: *I ask each couple who wish to marry to bring a symbolic meal to this occasion - to remind them that in the same sense that their bodies need to be nurtured daily, so does their love.*

I ask that they bring whatever is bread and wine to them, but it must be the real thing - their daily bread, no matter what it may be: toast, croissants, doughnuts... or bran flakes...

I ask them to bring their celebratory drink - whatever they will use to toast each other on their first anniversary and on all important occasions...

I ask them to bring a plate for the daily bread and either one cup or two. These utensils should be ones that either already have meaning for them or will become sacred to them by virtue of being used in this ceremony....

This particular couple chose to bring cinnamon toast, each in their preferred style.

---

[53] *Robert Fulghum - 'From Beginning to End: The Rituals of our Lives'* *(1995)*

To the couple: *Take a piece of the toast and feed one another that you may be reminded of your responsibility to nurture one another daily and that you may recognise and celebrate your differences. Take a taste from each other's style of cinnamon toast...*

There are two cups here... Drink to one another.

As long as you live, may you never be too busy to celebrate whatever great occasions come to your lives. May you have many reasons to drink from these vessels.

♡ Sharing wine is a popular wedding tradition, often using one cup.

Here are some words which give context to the ritual:

This cup of wine is symbolic of the cup of life. As you share the one cup of wine, you undertake to share all that the future may bring. All the sweetness life's cup may hold for you should be sweeter because you drink it together; whatever drops of bitterness it may contain should be less bitter because you share them.[54]

♡ Afghanistan - sugar water is blessed and offered to the couple to drink, affirming their intention to remain kind with each other.

♡ Shinto (Japan) - the ritual of drinking sake is a significant part of marriage proceedings. Once a couple have taken three sips from each of three cups three times, they are considered married.

♡ Korea - the couple drink a special white wine in reverential silence. The bride and groom first drink from their own cup, made from two halves of one

---

[54] *Rabbi Devon A. Lerner - 'Celebrating Interfaith Marriages' (1999)*

gourd. Then the wine from both cups is mixed together, symbolising two lives joining, and they drink again.

♡ China - the couple drink wine from two wedding cups tied together with a red ribbon. The first sip is taken individually, and the second after they have exchanged cups while crossing their arms.

♡ 'Coupe De Mariage' - French couples drink from a double-handled goblet, often in the family for generations, to demonstrate their intention to share all that lies ahead.

♡ Scottish 'Quaich'

This is a flat two-handled bowl: the Celtic cup of trust and friendship. Clan chiefs would drink from the same quaich, which was offered and received with both hands, proving neither held a weapon and the drink was not poisoned.

Couples may pour their individual drinks into the quaich, symbolising two lives merging.

Expressing Union/Joining

Many such rituals include tying some sort of material, giving us the term 'tying the knot,' synonymous with 'getting married.'

♡ Knots - Some say the tradition of 'tying the knot' comes from ancient Babylon, where threads from the couple's clothing were ceremonially tied together. Others believe the term originates from the old Celtic tradition of Handfasting (see below).

Russia - knots were considered protective. Fishing nets, being full of knots, were thrown over the bride for good fortune.

Cambodia - Knots for good luck are tied on a string bracelet by the couple's parents and grandparents and given to the newlyweds to end the ceremony.

♡ Philippines - The bride's veil is pinned to her groom's shoulder as a symbol of their union.

♡ Thailand - A garland of flowers is linked around a couple's joined hands.

♡ The Pipe - Smoking the sacred pipe is an essential way of connecting with Spirit within many Native American traditions. In the context of a wedding, the smoke carries a couple's intentions into the universe.

Handfasting

Some suggest this term comes from Old Norse '*hand-festa,*' meaning 'to join hands.' 'Handfasting' is thought to derive from 'hand-fastening', or the idea of making fast a pledge.

The actual binding of hands seems to have originated in medieval Scotland and Ireland and likely denoted betrothal. In time, it became a form of legally-binding marriage. This continued in Scotland until as late as 1940

Handfastings were also recognised as a 'trial marriage,' allowing a couple to live together for a year. They were once commonplace and often agreed to at the summer Lammas fairs. They would be married at the same fair the following year if they chose.

Many couples today choose to include a handfasting ritual as part of their wedding ceremony. Below are some of the ideas and wordings I have used.

♡ The material used can be significant for some. To consider:

- Two ribbons/cords represent each partner and all that they bring. Scottish couples often use a strip of their family tartans.

- Different coloured ribbons representing particular qualities, eg. red for passion, blue for calm, yellow for joy etc.

- Ivy - symbolic of togetherness and longevity, used in wedding rites since Roman times.

- Red thread or cord dipped in holy water - used in Cambodia and other Buddhist cultures. Red represents life, passion, joy and good fortune. Water symbolises life and purity.

♡ Hands can be tied several times, representing whatever you would like. Eg. for the bride, for the groom, for love or the relationship itself.

♡ If the hand-fasting is incorporated into the vow-taking section, each time a vow is made, hands can be bound to seal the intent.

♡ Some wordings for this part of the ritual:

1. *With this ribbon, I join you one to the other:*
   I join you in communion of body, mind, heart, and spirit
   I join you in equality and friendship
   I join you in the love that unifies all
   So are you joined.

2. *Please give one another your right hand. This represents the strengths and gifts you each bring to your marriage. And now your left - symbolic of the vulnerabilities and areas of growth that you both bring. All is included in this marriage. Together, your hands form the infinity symbol -*

113

strong and whole and complete, the symbol of a
love that will go on forever.

3. *'Now join your hands, and with your hands your
   hearts.'* (Shakespeare)

4. 'Blessing of the Hands' by Rev Daniel L. Harris

*These are the hands of your best friend, young
and strong and full of love for you, that are
holding yours on your wedding day.*

*These are the hands that will work alongside
yours as you build your future together.*

*These are the hands that will passionately love
you and cherish you through the years, and with
the slightest touch, will comfort you like no other.*

*These are the hands that will hold you when fear
or grief fills your mind.*

*These are the hands that will give you strength
when you struggle and support and
encouragement to chase down your dreams.*

*These are the hands that will tenderly hold your
children and help keep your family together as
one.*

*These are the hands that will, countless times,
wipe the tears from your eyes, tears of sorrow,
and tears of joy.*

*And lastly, these are the hands that, even when
wrinkled with age, will still be reaching for yours,
still giving you the same unspoken tenderness
with just a touch.*[55]

---

[55] *I sourced this from a Google search; there are slightly differing versions
out there. I don't know which is the original, but the essence is the same.*

♡ Blood Ties

Some cultures required the ritual exchange of blood – literally merging two bloodlines.

- Afghanistan - a couple's palms were dipped in henna and held together, reminiscent of the ancient practice of cutting their palms to mix their blood.

- Romany traveller communities - sometimes a couple mingled their blood or ate a cake with a few drops of their blood in it.

♡ Marital Blanket, Shawl or Cloak

Exchanging a shawl or blanket can represent the protection and shelter being offered. In some traditions, a shawl around the wedding pair symbolises that their marriage is wrapped in (God's) love, warmth and care.

In some Native American traditions, a couple are wedded under a special blanket and, once married, it is their blanket to keep them warm at night.

♡ Marriage/Unity Candle

This simple ritual works well with four candles. The first is lit at the beginning of the ceremony, representing Love, God, or the goodness of life, supporting us always.

At the appropriate time in the ceremony, the couple each light a candle from the central flame. These represent all that they each bring to the marriage. Then, using the flames from the two individual candles, the couple light the fourth candle together – their

Marriage or Unity Candle. This may be lit again on anniversaries or whenever love needs re-kindling.

Some example wording: *In times ahead, light this candle when peace and understanding are needed. It will shine a beacon of light and love, reminding you of the vows made here today and of the need to bring things into the open. In this Light, may all conflict be resolved and forgiven.*

- Moravia - the couple lights a large candle which is passed around. Each guest lights their own candle from it, symbolically filling the marriage with light.

♡ Salt Ceremony

Salt is a preservative and purifier, once highly prized. The couple each have some salt which they pour into one container, symbolising a life now shared. 'It also symbolises how love and marriage can enhance every aspect of the day-to-day life of a couple, in the same way as a pinch of salt can bring out the flavour of food.'[56]

♡ Unity Sand Ceremony

Again, this offers a strong visual image of the merging of lives in marriage. The couple each have different coloured sand, which they pour into a glass vessel. This can be a good way of including any children already present in the relationship, as they add their own coloured sand to the mix.

---

[56] *Jane Patmore – 'Celebrate your Love: How to create a unique, modern and personalised wedding ceremony' (2016)*

'Jumping the Broom' or 'Besom/Broomstick Weddings'

This old tradition has either been the marriage ritual in its own right or incorporated into a wider ceremony. Interestingly, it originates in two very different parts of the globe: pre-Christian Europe and also parts of Africa. It involves jumping over a broomstick, sometimes stuck aslant in a doorway, at others, lying on the ground or held higher.

West African traditions of jumping the broom were transported to America with slavery. Forbidden to marry, slaves devised their own clandestine ceremonies using their traditions from home.

In Europe, especially among the Celts, pagan marriages and Beltane trysts were often established with a leap over the broom. It remains popular within contemporary Wiccan and other earth-based traditions today.

This ritual can symbolise:

- The threshold the couple are crossing
- Setting up hearth and home
- The 'leap of faith' required in creating a new life together
- New life beginning with a 'clean sweep'
- Hurdles to be faced together

Acts of Ceremonial Washing / Purification / Transition

Many cultures include variations on the theme of washing or anointing a bridal couple's hands or feet. It denotes blessing, cleansing and a new, 'fresh' life.

♡ Thailand - a respected guest pours water from a conch shell over the couple's hands while wishing them a happy marriage

♡ Uganda - In a Batooro wedding, the couple enter a courtyard, undress and wash each other from a bowl of ice-cold water. This ritual ablution washes away the past to begin anew.

♡ !Kung San of the Kalahari (southern Africa) – in a similar gesture of transformation, the newlyweds here are anointed with oil, representing fertility, and red ocher as a symbol of life force.

♡ A couple may show their care and respect by washing and drying each other's hands or feet.

New Status

Marriage has traditionally marked adulthood and the responsibilities with it. Some wedding customs have included playful testing of a person's readiness for these obligations.

♡ Scotland - to prove his worth, a Highland groom was given a large basket (creel) of stones to carry through the village. This 'creeling' ceremony was completed by his bride coming out to kiss him.

♡ Croatia - after the vow-taking, a bride's female relatives would sing to her while replacing her wedding veil with a scarf and apron, the symbols of a wife.

♡ Hungary - the groom would give his bride a bag of money during the ceremony as a sign of his trust and care.

♡ Germany - the fun custom of 'log-sawing' often ended the ceremony. Using a long saw with two handles, the couple must saw through a log together. It represents their first obstacle, demonstrating their teamwork and how they will meet future challenges.

♡ African-American - the newlyweds cut a ribbon held by an elder of each of their families to demonstrate that they belong with each other now.

Symbols and Rituals of Fertility

Historically, marriage has been synonymous with the bearing and raising of children. Large families were considered the ultimate good fortune. It is no wonder that many wedding traditions include symbols of fertility and rituals invoking the arrival of children.

♡ Africa - in countries where cowrie shells are abundant, these symbolise fertility and are a popular wedding ornament.

♡ Korea - white geese are considered a symbol of fertility. Traditionally, the groom would ride to his bride's house on a white pony bearing a white goose. This has been replaced by a wooden goose today.

Similarly, a couple places a pair of ducks in their new home. The ducks facing each other denote marital harmony.

♡ Korea - the bride gives her new in-laws some dates and chestnuts, which represent children. They give her some sake and then throw the dates and chestnuts for her to catch in her wedding skirt.

♡ Jewish - the groom stamps on a pomegranate, spraying his feet and ankles with seed in a graphic display of virility.

♡ Croatia - guests walk around a well or water source three times, throwing apples into it to ensure luck and fertility for the newlyweds.

♡ Wheat has long symbolised abundance, harvest and therefore fertility. Many cultures include wheat bread in their wedding celebrations. An ancient fertility rite involved breaking bread over the bride's head. It was fortuitous for the guests to eat the crumbs of such a loaf.

A 'Nurturing the Marriage' Ritual

This 'Wine-Box Ritual' recognises the wedding ceremony as only the beginning of married life, which can be returned to as often as wanted.

The couple each write a letter describing what they love and appreciate about each other and their relationship. During the ceremony, the unread letters are locked in a box, along with a bottle of wine (or favourite drink).

At any point in the future - an anniversary or when the marriage needs nurturing - they can open the box, drink the wine and read what they have written to one another. This offers an opportunity to celebrate, reminisce and affirm their love and commitment.

Wine can be replaced and the box added to at any moment of inspiration, as the marriage changes over time.

♥ The Address/Charge

Typically called 'The Address', this part of the ceremony is an opportunity 'to address' the couple with words of wisdom and empowerment directly before their vows. I love the term 'The Charge' for the energy and potency it transmits.

Ideally, this message is given by someone steeped in presence and grace, able to channel the deepest of blessings, love and support so the couple may cross the threshold filled with inspiration and joy.

These words can be a mix of the personal, and of love and marriage more generally. They can be prepared in advance or expressed spontaneously, in the moment.

The personal message may draw on the couple's own story, highlighting their strengths and empowering their vision for the future. Using their own words (based on a questionnaire and getting to know them), I often remind a couple of what they love and appreciate about one another.

I have often used the words below, adapting where necessary to incorporate my own inspiration for the particular couple I am working with. Perhaps something here may uplift and nourish your vision of marriage:

1. From 'Illuminata' by Marianne Williamson

   I congratulate you on the journey of your lives, on the strength and the courage it has taken for each of you to make your way to this place. Both of you have found a way to put away childish things and embrace a very serious love. You receive on this day the blessing of this, for yourselves and for all the world.

We live in challenging times. This marriage is not to be an escape from the world, but indeed it is to be a commitment to greater service to the world. You shall not exclude the world but include it in your love. Together, in this marriage, you shall contribute more fully, for you shall be more full.

<u>Bride</u>, <u>Groom</u> is God's gift to you, but he is not a gift for you alone. In your love, may this man find within himself a greater sense of who he is meant to be. May you see the good in this man, accept him for who he is and who he shall be, that thus he might be healed and made strong. May this man find, literally, the kingdom of heaven through the love you share.

And so it is with you also, <u>Groom</u>, that although <u>Bride</u> is the Universe's gift to you, she is not intended for you alone. In your love, may she find herself so beautiful and strong and brave and true, that the whole world might be blessed by the presence of a woman who shines so. May she relax in your arms as she has never relaxed before.

May you both know that, from now on, there is one on whose love you can depend forever.

Our prayer for you both is that you might find in each other's love such profound acceptance and total release, that together you might experience the forgiveness that shall free the world. May you create, with God, a piece of heaven on earth.

To both of you, this is the time to release all impediments to your joy. In this moment, may you forgive each other any past transgressions that you might enter this marriage reborn. You are given the chance to begin your lives again this day, as the

Blessing of marriage and of the Universe grants you radical renewal through the power of this commitment.

You commit to a compelling future for yourselves, for any children you might one day have, and to any part you might play in the healing of the world...

2. Original source unknown

    Marriage is perhaps the greatest and most challenging adventure of human relationships. No ceremony can create your marriage; only you can do that - through love and patience; through dedication and perseverance; through talking and listening, helping and supporting and believing in each other; through tenderness and laughter; through learning to forgive, learning to appreciate your differences, and by learning to make the important things matter, and to let go of the rest. What this ceremony can do today is to witness and affirm the choice you have made to stand together as lifemates and partners.

3. From 'Joining Hands and Hearts' by Susanna Stefanachi Macomb

    You are the architects of your marriage. Let it be magnificent to behold! Let all who come into your home benefit from the warmth of its radiance. May it inspire others to love.

    Let your arms be a safe haven, a refuge for each of you to come home to every day. Drink from each other's inner well, and feel renewed, refreshed each and every day. Enjoy each other. Laugh much. Enjoy the process, the dance of life. Cherish your time together, for life is a gift. Be slow to anger and quick to forgive. Use kind and gentle words. Yes, even in the hard times – especially then, for the storms of life will inevitably come. It is then you are called upon to hold each other even closer.

Put your relationship on the altar of your lives and dedicate yourselves to it…

4. Original source unknown

    Remember that this wedding is only a symbol, a celebration, a public recognition of what already exists in the silent places of your hearts. It is your marriage and not something created by law or by religion - it is yours to define, yours to make real, yours to live. Nothing can make it anything more than what already exists in your hearts. Remember also that marriage is a shared relationship, not a matter of possession. It is a means of showing your commitment to one another, not a blind surrendering of personality. It is not an excuse to become limited in your outlook; it is an opportunity for mutual growth.

5. 'In my Heart' by Ashley Rice

    You don't have to be perfect to belong in this place. You don't have to have all the answers or always know the right thing to say. You can climb the highest mountain if you want. Or quietly imagine that you might someday. You can take chances or take safety nets, make miracles or make mistakes. You don't have to be composed at all hours to be strong here. You don't have to be bold or certain, to be brave or even know who you want to be…just take my hand and rest your heart and stay with me awhile.

6. From 'From Beginning to End' by Robert Fulghum

    Look at one another and remember this moment. Before this moment, you have been many things to one another - acquaintance, friend, companion, dancing partner, and even teacher, for you have learned much from one another in these last few years. Now you shall say a few words that take you across a threshold of life, and things will never quite be the same between you. For after these vows, you shall say to the world: this is my husband; this is my wife.

7.   Catherine Wright[57]

Through your commitment to each other, may you grow and nurture a love that makes both of you even better people, a love that continues to give you great joy, and also a passion for living that provides you with energy and patience to face the responsibilities of life. Loving someone is a reason to stretch beyond our limits.

♥ Vows

Declaring the promises, intentions, and most intimate truths of our hearts cross a couple over the threshold into marriage.

Below are some examples, each highlighting a slightly different aspect or view of marriage.

1.   This is a traditional form of wording:

Do you, ____, take ___ for your lawful wife/husband, to have and to hold, from this day forward, for better, for worse, for richer, for poorer, in sickness and health, until death do you part? - I do.

2.   The words 'accept', 'choose', 'take' and 'recognise' all have different nuances. This example also highlights

---

[57] *Catherine Wright - Interfaith Minister colleague and friend*

different perspectives around the longevity of marriage. Which wording feels most right for you?

Do you, ___ accept/choose/take/recognise ___ as your husband/wife?

Will you cherish and respect him/her with your heart and soul, offer him your friendship, care and support, honour his growth and freedom as your own, love him and embrace him through life's joys and challenges for as long as you both shall live/ until death do you part/ as long as your purpose is served/ as long as God/the Gods will it?
- I do/I will.

3. ____, *do you take ____ to be your wife/husband?*

   Do you promise to love her/him/them, comfort her, honour and protect her, and, forsaking all others, be faithful to her as long as you both shall live? - I do.

4. *Do you welcome conflict in the understanding that it creates an opportunity for renewal and deeper intimacy? - We do.*
   Do you welcome the other in their fullness, choosing them exclusively to play a unique part in your path to wholeness? - We do.

   Do you welcome the journey together, sharing equally the joys, the burdens and the responsibilities that come through partnership? - We do.

   Do you come here today to marry one another because of your trust in the love you have experienced together? - We do.
   - Inspired and based on vows written by Neil Douglas-Klotz[58]

---

[58] *Neil Douglas-Klotz - author and scholar in religious studies, psychology and spirituality*

5. *Do you vow to bring love and joy to this union? - I do.*

   Do you vow to honour that which you hold most sacred? -I do.

6. *Do you, ___, promise to love, ___? Do you promise to practice generosity, morality, patience, and joy in all you do; mindfulness and wisdom to treat ____ with loving-kindness and compassion, for all the time you are together, knowing that this commitment can only be as good as the two of you make it? - I do.*

7. This one includes bridesmaids and best men:

   Do you accept ___ as your husband/wife sincerely, in devotion? - I do.

   Will you consider this woman/man who is to be your wife/husband as the most sacred trust given to you (by God/in this life)? - I will.

   To best men/bridesmaids: Will you be witness to what ____ has promised?

   Each best man or bridesmaid: - I will.

♥ Exchange of Rings (or other objects)

Most cultures include the exchange of something tangible as an important part of the marriage rite. The exchange is often made between the bride and groom themselves, but sometimes between the parents and the marrying couple, or between the groom and his future in-laws.

The object may demonstrate a person's (supposed) worth or wealth or be a physical reminder of the marriage contract. This is often a ring, but across time and cultures, other objects have 'sealed the deal' as well. Whatever is used within the context of ritual takes on special meaning.

♡ Shoe - in ancient Egypt, the bride's father typically gave her shoes to the groom to seal the marriage contract.

There is a connection between shoes, marriage and luck even to this day, as seen in the tradition of tying shoes to the back of the bridal car.

♡ Coin - an ancient symbol of betrothal in many places. A man would break a coin in two, keeping one half himself and giving the other to his sweetheart.

♡ Fiji - the groom would give his in-laws a whale's tooth to prove his eligibility.

♡ A God/Goddess Gift - the bride, as representative of the goddess, gives her man a 'goddess gift' while he offers her a 'god gift' in return.

Wedding Ring History and Lore

The earliest evidence of wedding rings dates back nearly 5,000 years to Egypt. In 860, the pope decreed that a man must give his betrothed an engagement ring. By the Middle Ages, the ring had all but replaced the broken coin as a symbol of marriage.

Rings change according to fashion. A gold band is traditional today, but from the 1600s, gold rings with two clasped hands were popular for the next 300 years. Until the seventeenth century, 'spousing rings' were worn on the right hand, but during the Reformation, no rings were exchanged during the wedding ceremony itself.

The custom of exchanging rings during the ceremony began to be re-established in the 1600s. It was typically worn on the right hand in England. In 1690, the left hand was declared more appropriate. Protestant Germans, and other countries, still favour the right hand. It was not traditional to use a ring for marriage in Scotland at all.

The third finger of the left hand became the designated 'ring finger,' possibly linked to an ancient belief that this finger is directly connected to the heart by 'the vein of love.' Unless for warding off harm, a wedding ring should never be removed, lest bad luck follows.

Ring Styles, Symbolism, and Customs

♡ Gimmal/Gimmel Ring - of French origin, was popular in Renaissance times and used as a sign of friendship, love or betrothal. It is designed as two clasped hands made up of two or three parts that link together to form one complete ring. The name comes from the Latin word for 'twin.' In Elizabethan England, they were called 'joint rings.'

A betrothed couple each wore one part and, if there were three pieces, a close friend wore the third ring until the wedding day when it was finally assembled into one ring on the bride's finger.

♡ The Claddagh Ring - of ancient Ireland, this depicts two hands (friendship) holding a heart (love), with a crown (loyalty) above. Legend tells of a man forced overseas to labour. There he learnt the art of silver-smithing. Finally returning home, he found his sweetheart had never wed and joyfully crafted the now famous Claddagh wedding band for her.

♡ Sweden - a bride traditionally wore three bands on her wedding finger. The first signified engagement, the second marriage, and the third motherhood.

♡ Some West African cultures - the husband wears a gold ring, representing the masculine and the sun, while the wife wears silver for femininity and the moon.

♡ Diamonds and Gold - nowadays, diamonds are the most popular engagement rings in the West. Diamonds represent transformation, having once been coal. Gold, representing the sun, symbolises good fortune and a bright future.

Coins and Prosperity

Traditionally, marriage signalled setting up home and preparing for a family. People gave generously to the newlyweds in any way they could.

In many cultures, giving coins during the marriage rite symbolises the prosperity and abundance hoped for the couple.

♡ Thirteen Coins *(Arras)* - originating in Spain, the tradition of 'arras' is now popular throughout Latin America. Traditionally, thirteen gold coins from the groom passed between the couple, ending up in the bride's hands. Clattering the coins was important – originally to keep harm at bay, now for fun and dramatic effect.

Nowadays, the ritual may symbolise abundance and a couple's willingness to care and provide for each other. Each coin can represent the Thirteen Values or Virtues of Marriage: love, peace, commitment, trust, respect, joy, happiness, nurturing, honesty, harmony, wholeness, faithfulness and co-operation. Sometimes thirteen coins are given as a blessing for every month of the year and one for luck.

♡ Italy - in the tradition known as 'Le Buste,' the bride carries a special pouch to receive envelopes of monetary gifts.

♥ The Pronouncement

There are different ways of declaring a couple married. In the first few examples below, the officiant assumes this authority. Number 5 has the guests declare themselves witness of a marriage having taken place, while the couple declare themselves married in the last two.

1. *As you have promised to love one another according to your sacred vows, it is with great joy that I now pronounce you husband and wife/married!*

2. *_____ & ____, you have been brought together by love and commitment. You have exchanged solemn and sacred vows. By this integrity and truth, in the beloved company of family and friends, it is my honour to pronounce you husband and wife.*

3. *Your friends and family, all of us here, rejoice in your happiness and we pray that this day marks only one of many more blessings you will share in the years ahead. And now that you have spoken the words and performed the rites that unite your lives, I do hereby, in accordance with your beliefs and the laws of this country, declare your marriage to be valid and binding, and I now declare you husband and wife.*

4. *In the name of all that is sacred and loving, I now pronounce you husband and wife*

5. *With great joy, we, your family and friends, pronounce you husband and wife!*

6. (Couple speaking together): *We declare ourselves married/ husband and wife!*
   (One at a time): *Please meet my wife/husband, Mr/Mrs_____!*

7. *From 'Conversations with God' by Neale Donald Walsch*
   We recognise with full awareness that only a couple can administer the sacrament of marriage to each other, and only a couple can sanctify it. Neither church, nor legal power invested in me, can grant me the authority to declare what only two hearts can declare, and what only two souls can make real.
   And so now, inasmuch as you, _____, and you, _____, have announced the truths that are already written in your hearts, and have witnessed the same in the presence of your friends and the One Living Spirit - we observe joyfully that you have declared yourself to be husband and wife.

♥ The Kiss

The 'official' kiss gives a non-verbal seal to the vows and pronouncement that have just taken place. It is generally their very first act as a married couple.

The origins of the 'first kiss' actually began with the priest! To bless a marriage inside the church, the priest gave a holy 'kiss of peace' to the groom, who then gave one to his bride. This led to the familiar phrase 'You may now kiss the bride.'

Though deeply rooted in Anglo-Saxon-based cultures today, the kiss is not universally associated with marriage. It does not belong to traditional Swedish wedding customs, for example, let alone further afield in Africa or Asia.

♡ Polynesian 'Honi' - in this ancient greeting, two people touch foreheads and then press noses together, inhaling at the same time. In this intimate act, breath and life force is shared. This 'kiss' can be a lovely addition to a wedding ceremony.

♥ Affirmation of the Community

This is an alternative to the 'Guest Declarations' described earlier and works well after the couple have said their vows.

For example: *Now that you have heard ___ & ___ exchange their vows, do you, their family and friends, promise to encourage and support them in creating a strong and vital marriage? - We do!*

♥ Closure

The purpose of whatever comes at this point in the ritual is to confirm, summarise and complete. There is a sense of Benediction. As the space was opened at the beginning, so it needs to be closed now. Anything that was called in needs to be released and thanked. A journey has taken place in which everyone present has shared.

Let's remember that even though the formal part of the day is over, the process continues. The 'invisible' workings may long keep unfolding, the treasures and wisdoms revealed needing time to integrate.

♥ Exit

♡ Church Bells - triumphantly mark the closure of a formal wedding ceremony, announcing for all the world to hear: 'Some newlyweds are in our midst!'

♡ Confetti - guests exuberantly congratulate the newlyweds with a shower of good luck wishes and confetti. In olden times, cereal grains and nuts were used to ensure fertility. Rice is still popular in many parts of the world. German lore says that every grain that sticks in the bride's hair represents each child she will have. Coloured paper confetti became popular for a long time, but bubbles or petals make eco-friendly alternatives today.

♡ Germany - guests string ribbons across the door to block the exit of the newlyweds. They can only pass once the promise of a party has been extracted.

♡ Making Noise - In many traditions, loud noise was believed to ensure good luck and ward off evil. People were deemed particularly susceptible at threshold moments, hence its significance.

   • Vestiges of these old ideas have continued to this day with smashing crockery, banging saucepans and honking car horns. Old tin cans clatter behind the bridal car (UK). Passing cars often honk back for good luck, adding to the general cacophony.

   • Processions of loud instruments - drums, brass and horns - often lead the bridal party and/or their guests to or from a wedding.

   • Fireworks - in some parts of the world, eg. China, firecrackers and fireworks are an integral part of wedding celebrations.

CHAPTER TEN

Post-Ceremony Traditions

'Pause' after the Ceremony

Although this tradition is more fully explained in the chapter on religious customs, the Jewish concept of *Yichud* (meaning 'seclusion') seemed so important that I wanted to highlight it here.

Essentially, this is a short time allocated to the couple to be alone together, after the ceremony and before the festivities begin.

Lucky Charms

There has long been a sense of wonder and mystery around a new bride. Archetypally, a woman is transformed on her wedding day, elevating her from mortal to Queen or Goddess.

In times of old, the bride-goddess was attributed magical properties, and simply being in her proximity was fortuitous. Country lore reflects the ancient appreciation of her life-generating power.

♡   Since the ancient worship of the Great Mother goddesses of fertility, harvest and abundance (eg.

Demeter and Ceres), there has been a strong link between brides and fecundity. Right up until the early twentieth century, farmers asked brides to bless their crops to ensure a plentiful harvest.

♡ In Scotland and other places, it was auspicious to get the first kiss from the bride the moment the ceremony was over. Young men vied for the privilege.

♡ Chimney Sweeps - In Britain, it was good luck for the bride to kiss and the groom to shake hands with a chimney sweep on their wedding day.

♡ Bees - once considered 'divine messengers,' country folk shared any significant news with the family bees. Brides gave them cake and beer to ensure her future fertility and happiness.

♡ Feeding the cat - a bride would feed the cat before leaving her old home.

Feasting, Drinking and Merry-Making - The Wedding Reception

Feasting, singing and dancing, toasting and speech-making, pranks and games are vital elements of weddings the world over. Even the economically-poorest communities celebrate a wedding with gusto and generosity.

It is the spirit of goodwill and joyous celebration that counts. The sense of belonging and well-being within a community is strengthened by such events. The newlyweds begin married life buoyed up by the energy and good wishes of all who love them, with a host of joyful memories to feast upon in the years to come.

♡ Poland - newlyweds are welcomed at the reception by their parents offering them bread and salt. Bread represents abundance and salt, the overcoming of any hardships.

♡ Chinese Tea Ceremony - newlyweds traditionally served tea to each guest, officially establishing their place within the family. The couple's ancestors were believed to witness them performing this ancient and important marriage rite.

Dancing

The newlyweds tend to lead or perform the first dance.

♡ UK - the bride shares a dance with her father, and the groom with his new mother-in-law. These small yet significant ritualised acts demonstrate both the bonds and the changes in their relationship.

♡ Finland - the bride often wears a golden crown. At the reception, she is blindfolded by her bridesmaids for the 'Dance of the Crown.' The young women dance around the bride, and whoever's head she places the crown on will be the next to wed.

♡ Finland - a plate is placed on the bride's head for the first dance. When the plate falls and breaks, the number of pieces indicate how many children a couple will have.

Wedding Cake

Wedding cakes date back at least as far as Roman times. They were originally broken over the couple's heads for luck and fertility. Guests also sprinkled themselves with the crumbs for good fortune.

This custom was replaced by eating the cake at the celebrations. It had to be tasted by all present, to share the good luck. Maidens would place a crumb under their pillow to dream of their future husband.

Wedding cakes have varied in style from country to country. Here are two examples:

♡ UK - the tradition of tiered and iced cakes reached Britain via France after 1660. The bride took no part in making or tasting the cake before her wedding. On the day, it took pride of place throughout the reception. Traditionally, the bride made the first cut to ensure a happy, child-filled marriage. Nowadays, newlyweds cut the cake together. The first, and largest tier, is shared amongst the guests, the middle tier given to those unable to attend, and the third saved for the first baby's christening.

♡ France - the *croquembouche* (*'crunch in the mouth'*), invented by a pastry chef in the late 1700s, has become a classic French wedding cake. It is a tall pyramid of profiteroles, flamboyantly presented at dessert time. Guests chant for the cake (*'Le gateau! Le gateau!'*) and it is carried in, often sparkling with fireworks.

Toasting

Toasting is very likely 'a secular vestige of ancient sacrificial libations in which a sacred liquid was offered to the gods'[59] to ensure their favour.

---

[59] Dwight B. Heath (1995) 'International Handbook on Alcohol and Culture' from *https://culture.pl/en/article/a-foreigners-guide-to-polish-weddings*

Toasting in Europe dates back to the sixteenth century, when it was common to add toast to wine. Spiced stale bread made inferior wine more palatable. When toasting evolved into the tradition of honouring a person, they were often given the actual wine-soaked toast at the end.

Toasting became so popular in the seventeenth and eighteenth centuries that the role of 'Toastmaster' emerged to curb excessive toasting and drinking and preserve some decorum.

Other parts of the world have their own venerable toasting traditions. Those from Georgia, and other areas of the Caucasus region, date back some two and a half thousand years.

The Georgian *tamada* or 'toastmaster' plays a prominent role at any celebration to this day. It is an art passed down the generations, involving entertaining the guests with toasts and jokes, games and contests.

♡   Russia - the first toast is to the newlyweds. As soon as the guests shout *'Gorko, gorko!'* ('bitter') the couple must kiss to remove the bitterness from the vodka. Bitter is replaced by sweet, and the kiss continues as long as the chanting. The second toast is traditionally made to the parents.

Games, Contests and Pranks

In many countries, playing pranks on the newlyweds is considered a key component of any proper wedding. This does not feature as strongly in the English-speaking world.

♡   Georgia – Singing and dancing contests are popular. Eg. The bride's guests start singing until stopped by the toastmaster. The groom's guests resume singing, starting with the same word that the first group finished with. This continues until one side can go no further, and the toastmaster issues them a forfeit.

Eg. couples dance together on a small piece of paper. To ensure success, the men carry their partners, so it becomes a competition of strength.

♡ Mischief in the bridal suite - In many European countries (eg. Germany, Holland, Spain), friends cause havoc in the bed-chamber. They might, for instance, dismantle the bed, fill the room with balloons, or hide numerous alarm clocks.

♡ Tossing the Garter/Bouquet

In the fourteenth century, the bride tossed her garter for the men to catch. This bawdy tradition was gradually replaced by the bride throwing her bouquet for the unmarried women. Whoever caught it was supposedly next to wed.

♡ 'Kidnapping the Bride' - the playful versions of this custom that exist today very likely have their roots in much darker history. While not condoning non-consensual marriage, these examples illustrate the mischievous spirit of some wedding traditions.

• Germany - guests 'kidnapped' the bride and whisked her away to a local pub. On finding her, the groom must pay for the kidnapper's drinks to claim his new wife back.

• Georgia - 'stealing' the bride marks the climax of the entire wedding ceremony. The toastmaster may distract the groom while the bride is secreted away. The groom must then win her back. Alternatively, any guest(s) may steal the bride and demand a symbolic ransom from her new husband.

Threshold, New Home and Status Rites

The threshold of a home has long carried magical connotations. Romans and others believed it attracted harmful spirits or energies, particularly on significant occasions, such as birth, death and marriage.

A whole body of country lore grew up around these folk beliefs. Essentially, it was bad luck for a bride to touch the threshold as she entered her new home for the first time. Hence the tradition of the groom carrying his bride over the doorstep. Nowadays, it can be a playful start to married life.

♡ Ancient Greece - arriving at his family home, the groom lifted his bride from the carriage to be welcomed by her new mother-in-law carrying celebratory torches. The new wife burnt the axle of the carriage, symbolically severing herself from her childhood home. Then she was offered figs, dates and nuts, representing fertility and prosperity.

♡ Roman weddings ended with the bride being pulled away from her mother, marking the end of childhood. She was then led to her new home in a joyous procession. Once there, she made an offering by the door to demonstrate her new status. Her husband then helped her across the threshold while both repeated their wedding vows.

A wealthy bride was led to her new home by the vestal virgins, carrying a special cake. She carried a distaff, spindle and wool, symbolic of her wifely duties.

♡ The womb and phallus were held sacred and, up until the fourteenth century, it was common for a home to display representations of each. A symbolic phallus, sacred to the god, would be at the threshold of a home, ensuring blessing and fertility. The cauldron and hearth at the centre of the home represented the womb and was sacred to the goddess.

♡ Medieval times - the first ritual duty of a new wife was to make offerings to the household gods and to bring salt, bread and a new broom with her. Her mother-in-law handed her pokers and tongs, for the new wife was now mistress of hearth and home.

♡ Scotland - a new wife was welcomed by her mother-in-law. As she crossed the threshold, bread and cheese were held above her, or an oatmeal cake was broken over her head.

The groom's mother handed her daughter-in-law house keys, the furniture, tongs or a besom. The new mistress then lit the fire or swept the hearth.

A prayer was offered - 'may the Almighty make this woman a good wife.' The final ritual was to press the bride's hand into flour or oatmeal to ensure the household never went hungry.

♡ Sudan - at the new home, an egg is broken and the groom pronounced master of the house. Seven broomsticks are also burnt, symbolising a clean start.

♡ Poland - weddings culminated on the stroke of midnight with the ritual removal of the bride's veil. Her hair was then unbraided and cut, transforming her from a maiden into a wife. She was then presented with a special wedding cap.

The Wedding Night

♡ Scotland - 'Bedding the Bride' or the ceremony of *Beddan* was once commonplace and completed the wedding rites. Essentially, all the guests ended up in the marital bed-chamber, where toasts were made and items of the bride's clothing playfully fought over.

♡ Rural France - unmarried friends invaded the wedding night by turning up with champagne and chocolates, served in a chamber pot.

♡ Roman times - the marital bed-chamber was lit by sacred hawthorn torches.

♡ Ancient Greece - A friend of the groom guarded the bed-chamber, while the bride's friends sang special songs to support and protect her and invoke the blessings of pregnancy.

♡ Tudor England – the bride's mother made a special wedding quilt embroidered with good-luck symbols and the star signs of the couple. She also ensured the bed faced East-West.

Honeymoon

This literally means 'honey month' and describes the ancient tradition of newlyweds drinking honey wine or mead for a full moon cycle following their wedding. Honey was considered an aphrodisiac, and mead was known as the golden elixir, ambrosia, and nectar of the gods. It was believed to have magical properties linked to longevity, virility and fertility. As such, newlyweds were given a month's supply of honey wine to ensure multiple offspring.

Nowadays, the honeymoon is essentially a holiday, a concept reflected in some languages, eg. German *Hochzeitsreise* and French *Vacance de noces*, both meaning 'wedding holiday'.

As an integral part of the wedding rite, it allows a couple to recuperate after their wedding and its preparations and start integrating their experiences. It offers a short transition period before the return to everyday life, now as a married couple.

CHAPTER ELEVEN

Faith Traditions and Perspectives on Marriage

Most religions view marriage as a life-long sacrament. The word itself expresses a sense of 'making sacred,' a reminder that our relationships can be 'sanctified' places of love, havens of kindness.

Baha'i

♡ Marriage is considered 'a fortress for well-being and salvation' (Baha'u'llah). A married couple should be 'loving companions and comrades and at one with each other for time and eternity.'

♡ Couples can choose their partner, but parental permission is needed for marriage. Inter-racial marriages are encouraged as they demonstrate our core humanity.

♡ The core elements of a Baha'i wedding are very simple. Before two witnesses, the couple each repeats: 'We will all verily abide by the Will of God.'

♡ Divorce is allowed, but 'a year of patience' is encouraged; twelve months of living separately to reflect or attempt reconciliation.

♡ Humanity has two wings – the male and the female. If the wings are not equally matched the bird will not fly.[60]

Buddhism

♡ Historically, Buddhism viewed marriage as a hindrance to enlightenment. It still tends to be celebrated more as a social contract than a religious rite, although the blessings and guidance of monks are central.

♡ Weddings typically take place at the couple's home or local temple.

♡ Couples are encouraged to follow the Buddhist teachings of compassion, respect, kindness and harmony. They are joined 'mind to mind, body to body, nature to nature, and true nature to true nature.'

♡ Typical traditions include:

- an altar with candles, incense, flowers, water, fruits, sweets, or perfumed water.
- sprinkling the couple with blessed water.
- chanting of sacred texts.
- sounding bells at prominent places in the ceremony.
- the ceremony begins with the couple lighting candles and incense and offering flowers
- one candle is lit for the Buddha, another for the community of monks.

---

[60] *Abdu'l-Baha, in 'The Promulgation of Universal Peace'*

- scented water and flower petals may be sprinkled (on the earth or in a bowl) to represent beauty, love, compassion etc., the very foundation of the marriage and way of life.
- handfasting - using a silk scarf or Buddhist prayer beads.
- water - poured over the couple's joined hands to bless and purify.
- blessing and exchange of rings followed by words of benediction.
- white silk scarves - the ceremonial 'khata' are exchanged to end the ceremony as a sign of gratitude and respect.

Readings and Inspirations

1. We nourish ourselves and each other in living by the following five precepts:
   In every way we can, we allow our deepest self to appear.
   We take full responsibility for our own life in all its infinite dimensions.
   We affirm our trust in the honesty and wisdom of our own body, which with our love and reverence, always shows us the true way.
   We are committed to embrace all parts of ourselves, including our deepest fears and shadows, so that they can be transformed into light.
   We affirm our willingness to keep our hearts open, even in the midst of great pain
   - Zen Centre of San Francisco, adapted by Vicki Chang

2. Let us vow to remember the causes of suffering and to practice an end to suffering. I shall accept all that I cannot change and let my heart be broken.

May we be gentle all our days, here, there and everywhere.

Let us vow to bear witness to the wholeness of life, realizing the completeness of each and every thing. Embracing our differences. I shall know myself as you, and you as myself. May we serve each other for all our days, here, there and everywhere.

Let us vow to open ourselves to the abundance of life. Freely giving and receiving, I shall care for you, for the trees and stars, as treasures of my very own. May we be grateful for all our days, here, there and everywhere.

Let us vow to forgive all hurt, caused by ourselves and others, and to never condone hurtful ways. Being responsible for my actions, I shall free myself and you. Will you free me too? May we be kind all our days, here, there and everywhere.

Let us vow to remember that all that appears will disappear. In the midst of uncertainty, I shall sow love. Here! Now! I call to you: Let us together live the Great Peace that we are. May we give no fear for all our days, here, there and everywhere.

> *- 'A Blessing for the Journey' by Wendy Egyoku Nakao*

3. Today we promise to dedicate ourselves completely to each other, with body, speech, and mind.In this life, in every situation, in wealth or poverty, in health or sickness, in happiness or difficulty, we will work to help each other perfectly.The purpose of our relationship will be to attain enlightenment by perfecting our kindness and compassion toward all sentient beings.

> *- Lama Thubten Yeshe*

Christianity

♡ In the fifteenth century, marriage became one of the Christian 'seven sacraments' marking the major life events from birth to death.

♡ Eastern Orthodox - marriage is viewed as a union with God rather than a legal contract.

♡ Baptists - marriage is considered a covenant between the couple and God.

♡ Mennonites and Amish - believe that God willed marriage for companionship, procreation and raising a family. Divorce is considered a violation of God's will.

♡ Quaker - to be legal, an external authority is necessary, but the principle of a couple declaring *themselves* married in front of God and their community is important.

Traditions

Catholic and Protestant

♡ Groom, supported by his 'best man', waits with the minister at the front of the church.

♡ Guests stand as the bride enters, accompanied by her father. The bridal party may include 'flower girls,' 'pageboys' and bridesmaids.

♡ Bride stands to Groom's left, their backs to congregation, facing the minister and the altar.

♡ Friends of the bride sit on the left, the groom's on the right.

♡ Bride wears white, perhaps a veil, and carries a bouquet.

♡ Altar may have bread, wine and unity candles

Orthodox

♡ Marriage consists of two rites, performed back-to-back: the Betrothal followed by the Crowning.

♡ No vows are exchanged

♡ Objects on the altar include scriptures, the priest's blessing cross, a cup of wine, wedding candles, marriage crowns, rice and sugared almonds

♡ Russian Orthodoxy favours golden crowns, the Greek tradition uses flower wreaths.

♡ Bride wears white, and both bride and groom have attendants who assist them throughout the ceremony and carry the marriage crowns.

♡ The ceremony itself:

1. The Betrothal - takes place in the vestibule, where the priest recites prayers and blessings for every aspect of marriage.
2. The couple exchange rings by passing them between their right and left hands three times before ending up on the right-hand ring finger.
3. Chants, prayers and incense follow as the jubilant procession is led into the heart of the church for the marriage ceremony.
4. Lit candles, representing the light of Jesus, are given to the couple, and the three Great Prayers of Marriage are recited.
5. The Crowning Ceremony - Psalm 128 (extolling the joys of marriage) is sung, or a blessing

repeated three times, as the wedding crowns go back and forth between the couple's heads before settling in their rightful places.

6. Closure – the priest leads the newlyweds three times around the altar in a procession called 'the Dance of Isaiah.' This represents the course of married life, the circle of life itself, 'which finds its beginning and end in holy things.'[61]

Readings and Inspirations

1. Almighty God, you have made the bond of marriage a holy mystery. Hear our prayers for __ & __, who have come here today to be united in marriage. With faith in you and in each other, they pledge their love today. May their lives bear witness to the reality of that love.
   - Catholic invocation, adapted

2. We are gathered together in the sight of God to join this man and this woman in marriage. Let all who enter marriage know it as a sacred and joyous covenant, a way of life ordained by God from the beginning of creation. God blesses the covenant of marriage: that husband and wife may give to each other companionship, help and comfort, both in prosperity and in adversity; that they may hold sacred the expression of natural affections; that children may be born and nurtured in families; and that human society may stand on firm foundation. Let us therefore invoke the blessing of God on this marriage between __ & __.
   - Protestant invocation, adapted

---

[61] *Philip Zaleski and Paul Kaufman - 'Gifts of the Spirit: Living the Wisdom of the Great Religious Traditions' (2009)*

3. Marriage is a religious act, and the love that unites man and woman is part of the great love of God.

    - Ruth Midgley, from 'Quaker Faith & Practice'

4. The wedding is an act of worship, and not merely a formal indication in a register office. A Christian puts his vows into the hand of God, trusting that God will hold the couple where he wants them held. To turn a wedding into worship is to recognise that marriage is bigger than we are; that it is not just a pleasant arrangement we have made for our own convenience, but a vocation into which we have been drawn by nature and by God.

    - Harold Loukes, from 'Quaker Faith & Practice'

Confucian/Chinese

Marriage is negotiated between the two families and a matchmaker. Gifts and documents are exchanged, containing the 'eight characters' of the son and daughter, which includes the date and time of their births. The bride-to-be honours the gods and spirits of her ancestors at the family altar.

Readings and Inspirations

1. When two people are at one in their inmost hearts, they shatter even the strength of iron or bronze. And when two people understand each other in their inmost hearts, their words are sweet and strong, like the fragrance of orchids.

    - From the 'I Ching'

2. Ancient Chinese legend declares that two people are connected at birth by an invisible red thread. The

thread shrinks over the years until the couple is brought together in marriage. Nothing can sever this thread; marriage is their destiny.

Hinduism

♡ Marriage is considered the greatest of Hinduism's sixteen *samskaras*, or life-cycle rituals. It is viewed as a life-long sacred union, which enhances the spiritual development of both people. An individual alone cannot achieve enlightenment.

♡ The central rite takes place under a sacred canopy, where the couple are considered deities for the duration of the ceremony. Local custom varies, but the bride may become the goddess Parvati, and the mortal man at her side the god Shiva.

♡ The giving of one's child in marriage is considered the greatest gift.

♡ Traditionally, marriages have been arranged, with astrological compatibility taken seriously.

Traditions

♡ An astrologer sets an auspicious date. Four months of the year were unfavourable (roughly mid-July to November) as it is said Lord Vishnu sleeps then.

♡ Weddings are held after sunset and conducted by Brahmin priests in Sanskrit, the ancient 'language of the Gods,' and not in everyday use.

♡ Hindu weddings are elaborate, extending over several days, even weeks. The marriage process includes preparation rituals, honouring relevant deities at each partner's home, meals and gifts for the parents, separate parties for bride and groom, the marriage ceremony itself, followed by a lavish banquet.

♡ The rite has included a formal farewell of the bride by her family and friends as, traditionally, it was expected that she now belongs to her husband's household. This can be intensely emotional, almost as if she has 'died' to her family of origin.

♡ *Solah shringar* – an ancient code prescribing sixteen items of bridal wear: sari, bindi (red dot on the forehead), gold necklaces, earrings, flowers in the hair, bracelets, anklets, toe rings, perfumes, sandalwood paste for the skin etc. The bride also wears a tiny pendant of the goddess Lakshmi on her forehead to invoke prosperity.

♡ *Mandap* – the sumptuous wedding canopy, under which are two throne-like chairs for the couple, the sacred fire and an altar.

Possible Symbolism:

- Shelter, safety, peace, sanctity of the home.
- A womb of re-birth - bride and groom enter as individuals and are reborn a married couple.
- Open sides - the welcome that is always available to friends and family.

The actual marriage ceremony typically lasts 2-3 hours and includes various elements, some of which are almost mini ceremonies in their own right. Guests come and go freely during this time.

1. The Welcome Ceremony - the groom arrives with his family and is ritually welcomed. The bride's mother

marks his head with red powder, offers him honey, sweets and water or showers him with rice and flowers.

2. Invocation - Ganesha, the elephant god of wisdom, good luck and remover of all obstacles, is invoked.

3. Offering the Bride - both parents place their daughter's right hand in the groom's hands. Both parents are acknowledged by this gesture, and the bride is 'offered' as the most precious of gifts. Water may be poured from the hands of the bride's parents to the bride's hands, then to the groom's hands in a gesture of love and blessing flowing from one generation to the next.

4. The couple pledge themselves to each other by placing a red dot on each other's forehead.

5. The groom stamps on a clay pot wrapped in cloth, symbolising his strength and ability to overcome challenges.

6. Joining of Hands/Tying a Knot/Binding with cord symbolising two lives joining - the couple's hands are either tied with a thread, or a string is looped around their necks, or loose ends of their clothing are tied together.

7. Seven Steps and the Sacred Fire

♡ The fire is lit and offerings made, including prayers, flowers for beauty, coconut for fertility, rice for nourishment, ghee to feed the fire, sandalwood, and sweets for a sweet life.

♡ Four stones may be placed around the Fire, representing our highest aspirations:

Dharma – living a good life of wisdom and integrity
Artha – striving for happiness
Kama – nurturing a passion for life, family, children

Moksha – seeking spiritual wholeness

♡ Walking the Seven Steps (*Saptapadi*) - the couple take seven steps while circling the fire, as they make seven promises to each other. This act is at the heart of the Hindu wedding ritual and, once completed, the couple are considered married.

8. Touching Hearts - bride and groom place their hands on each other's hearts.

9. Gifting the Bride - the groom places a special necklace around his bride's neck, representing marriage.

10. Exchange of flower garlands - this traditional Asian ritual honours any special event. Here it signifies mutual respect and acceptance of the marriage.

11. Red powder - the groom or female relatives put red powder on the bride's forehead and in the parting of her hair. This marks her new status as a wife - red is the most auspicious colour and forbidden to unmarried women.

12. Communal Blessing - guests shower the newlyweds with petals, rice or confetti.

13. To end the ceremony, couples may glance at the never-moving pole star, symbolic of steadfastness and constancy.

Readings and Inspirations

1. May the nights be honey-sweet for us.
May the mornings be honey-sweet for us.
May the plants be honey-sweet for us.
May the earth be honey-sweet for us and the heavens be honey-sweet for us.

May the sun be all honey for us.

May the cows yield us honey-sweet milk.

As the heavens are stable, as the earth is stable, as the mountains are stable, as the whole universe is stable, so may our union be permanently settled.

2. It is not for the love of a husband that a husband is dear;

    but for the love of the soul in the husband that a husband is dear.

    It is not for the love of a wife that a wife is dear;

    but for the love of the soul in the wife that a wife is dear.

    It is not for the love of children that children are dear;

    but for the love of the soul in the children that children are dear.

    It is not for the love of all that all is dear;

    but for the love of the soul in all that all is dear.

    - Brihad-Aranyaka Upanishad

3. The Kama Sutra teaches that when the one man loves the one woman, and the one woman loves the one man, the angels abandon heaven and go to sit in that house and sing for joy.

4. Some contemporary wording for Walking the Seven Steps:

    i.   We shall cherish each other in sickness and health, in happiness and sorrow.

    ii. We shall be lifelong friends.

    iii. Together we shall share each other's ideals.

    iv. We shall nurture each other's strengths, talents and aspirations.

    v.   Together we shall make each other happy.

    vi. Together we shall love and care for our children and our families.

    vii. Together we will look toward the mysteries of the future with awe, open-mindedness and inspiration.

- Susannah Stefanachi Macomb, in 'Joining Hands and Hearts'

Islam

♡ Regarded as the norm, marriage is considered the foundation of society, a social responsibility, as well as a comfort and a gift from God.

♡ Although the Koran includes many rules concerning marriage, the wedding ceremony itself is not considered religious. The 'official' part is simple and informal, lasting just a few minutes and attended by immediate family only. The celebrations, however, may last for days.

♡ A sacred contract that legalises sexual relations.

♡ Mohammed taught that men and women are two halves that make a whole.

♡ Divorce is discouraged, though not forbidden. Mohammed exhorted: 'Get married, and do not divorce; indeed, divorce causes the Throne of God to shake!'

♡ The Koran says a man may have up to four wives as long as he treats each one fairly. Polygamy was perhaps a response to a battle in 625 when many women were left widowed.

Traditions

♡ Engagement can last anything from a day to several years. The couple were not permitted time alone together.

♡ Weddings do not take place during Eid, Ramadan or Yaum Ashura.

♡ The imam and two others witness the groom offering marriage and the bride accepting. A sermon or prayer may be included, but there are no vows, kisses, or ring exchange. Once the marriage contract (*nikah*) is signed, the marriage is legal.

♡ The wedding reception (*Walima*) often takes place on a different day to the legal ceremony, with men and women segregated. Alcohol is forbidden, as are music and dancing, if held in a mosque.

Readings and Inspirations

1. Praise be to Almighty God, the Merciful, the Compassionate. He created male and female, each in need of the other, and established the institution of marriage as a means of uniting two souls in a blessed bond of love.
   - Muhammad Abdul-Rauf, from 'Marriage in Islam'
   (adapted)

2. When a couple unite in marriage, God himself opens wide the heavens and commands legions of angels to go forth and bear witness to the miraculous act: two people have fallen in love, and the heavens sing and dance in celebration. All heaven rejoices for them.

3. When a man looks upon his wife and she upon him, God looks mercifully on them. When they join hands together, their sins disappear in the interstices of their fingers. When they love, the angels encircle the earth.
   - Mohammed, From 'One River, Many Wells' by
   Matthew Fox

Judaism

♡ Marriage is viewed as a divine command (a *mitzvah* or 'holy obligation'), expected of all Jews, and a sacred bond between a couple. It is considered natural, desirable, and a path of personal fulfilment.

♡ The Hebrew word for marriage, *kiddushin,* means 'sanctification.' Marriage offers a fresh start, with past transgressions absolved.

Traditions

♡ Typically spectacular and celebrated with hundreds of guests, Jewish weddings include many elements, ranging from the raucous, contemplative and explicit welcome of sacred presence. They begin with the announcement of intent to marry and end with seven days of celebration.

♡ Traditionally, weddings took place outside 'under the stars.' For centuries, the third day of the week (Tuesday) was considered especially fortuitous for weddings, as in the Creation story, the phrase '...and God saw that it was good' is mentioned twice in relation to this day.

♡ Orthodox custom dictates that a couple be apart for the week before the wedding.

♡ It was once customary to invite poor people to a wedding celebration to ensure good luck by bestowing generosity and abundance. For similar reasons of sharing hospitality and goodwill, it was also common to seek out a stranger.

♡ On the wedding day, the couple fast until after the ceremony.

♡ The absence of jewellery shows that inner virtue is prized more highly than the external.

♡ On the wedding morning, the bride and groom host separate receptions for the female and male guests respectively.

♡ *Bedeken* ('veiling') - the groom visits his bride before the ceremony, where he covers her face with a veil. Both sets of fathers and grandfathers then bless the bride in readiness for the ceremony.

♡ Marriage Contract *(Ketubah)* - Originally, this was the legal document, which particularly protected the wife's rights. It now signifies a spiritual covenant, usually signed immediately before the ceremony.

♡ Men and women are segregated for the ceremony itself within Orthodox tradition.

♡ *Chuppah* - the essential four-poled wedding canopy under which the ceremony is held. Often very elaborate and sumptuous, the early canopies were erected in the desert for the wedding night. It is either carried in or already in position. Being a pole bearer is a great honour.

♡ A typical ceremony includes the following elements:

   1. Entrance procession: once the canopy is in place, the groom is accompanied there by a parent on each side. The bride walks down the aisle with both her parents to join them. The rabbi often leads the procession.

   2. Circling - traditionally, the bride walked around the groom three or seven times, but nowadays, the

161

couple often choose to circle each other. Both numbers are considered mystical. The steps may represent the new life ahead. Esoterically, they signify the couple entering the seven spheres of each other's souls.

3. The Seven Blessings (*Sheva Brachot*) - central to Jewish wedding tradition, this adapted excerpt summarises the essence of these ancient blessings[62]:

    The first blesses the wine. The couple then drink from one cup, signifying sharing everyday life as well as joy and celebration.
    The second and third celebrate creation, culminating in the blessing of marriage.
    The fourth is a challenge to fulfil the potential for creativity, blessing and peace.
    The fifth affirms that marriage is made up of both passion and friendship.
    The sixth blesses the couple as separate individuals choosing to join in marriage
    The seventh unites the couple in gladness, 'surrounded by ten shades of joy and a chorus of jubilant voices.'

4. Exchange of Rings – an old custom has the groom place the ring on his bride's left index finger. She moves it to her right ring finger to demonstrate her acceptance.

5. Vows - simple vows are declared in front of two witnesses.

---

[62] *From www.interfaithfamily.com*

6. Breaking of the Glass - the groom concludes the wedding ceremony by stamping on a glass wrapped in cloth. This symbolically ends the old life before beginning the new. Guests shout '*Mazel tov!*' showering the couple with congratulations and good wishes. The commotion distracts evil spirits away from the couple.

♡ *Yichud* ('Seclusion') - A Moment of 'Pause' - the newlyweds retreat to a 'seclusion room' immediately after the ceremony to have some time alone together. It allows 'official' breathing space before greeting their guests. It is a chance to end their fast and adorn jewellery if they choose. The abundance and goodness that marks married life can now begin.

♡ Gladdening the Bride - the men dance for the bride during the wedding feast, praising her beauty. It fills her with joy and was originally a *mitzvah* - a divine commandment - and, therefore, obligatory.

Readings and Inspirations

1. Each person transmits a light which reaches heaven. When two souls who are destined for each other find one another, their streams of light flow together and a single brighter light goes forth from their united being.
   - Ba'al Shem Tov, eighteenth century

2. As you go into the world as husband and wife, we call upon four angels to assist you upon the journey of your life together. To your right shall walk the angel Gabriel, who will give you strength. To your left is Michael, who shall protect you. Behind you is Raphael, who shall

heal you. And directly in front of you is Uriel, whose name means 'the Light of God.' He will guide your way.
- *Rabbi Joseph Gelberman, 'The Blessing of the Four Archangels'*

3. Traditional Jewish teachings are about bringing god into the picture – of everything. God is made present in a husband and wife's most intimate contact together, and that time is seen as a blessing. Having sex is seen as a 'mitzvah,' the fulfilment of a divine commandment, and is to be approached as delicately and with as much respect as one would approach any other occasion of worship.

    - Rabbi Zalman Schachter-Shalomi

4. We wish to be generous and giving with each other as we work to build a marriage that will enrich our lives.
    We are grateful for the love and support of our families and friends. We wish for good health and much happiness for all.
    We acknowledge that we are but two people in this vast world. We wish to respect the diversity and strength of all those with whom we share this planet.
    We acknowledge our great privilege in marrying here today and we wish to build a world in which all couples have the right to commit their lives to one another in the eyes of the law and their fellow citizens.
    We wish to appreciate and complement our differences, using them to enrich our relationship.
    We wish to create a home that is filled with joy and love, open to all.
    As we marry here today, we are exceptionally grateful for this moment of unity and happiness. We hope that our lives and our marriage may work towards making the world a better place for those less fortunate.

    - Rabbi Renee Feller (adapted)

5. Give pleasure to these beloved companions as you did to your creation in the Garden of Eden so long ago. Blessed are you God, who makes the hearts of this couple rejoice. Blessed are You God, Source of the universe, who has created each of these two people, their delight and their happiness, their rejoicing and singing and dancing and festivity, love and friendship, peace and pleasure. Oh God, may the voices of this celebration be heard in the streets of our cities and the hills of our countryside. May the words of this couple go out with gladness from their wedding huppah and may the music of their friends and guests surround them. Blessed are You God, who brings joy to the hearts of this couple.

- A contemporary English version of the Seventh Blessing, www.interfaithfamily.com

Native American Spirituality

♡ Marriage is called 'The Path of Beauty' in some traditions.

♡ Typically held outside.

♡ Facing East - the direction of the sunrise, which signifies new beginnings, new life, hope. The sun is revered as a manifestation of Great Spirit, the sacred source of all.

Traditions

♡ Ritual objects – eg. sage, sweet-grass or cedar for purification, drums, flutes, rattles, the sacred pipe, water, fire.

Drums or rattles create ritual space, while the circular drum represents the universe; its beat the pulse of life.

♡ Four or Seven Directions - these are North, South, East and West, and some traditions additionally honour Above, Below and the Sacred Centre, or Great Mystery, at the heart of all.

♡ The Four Elements - Earth, Air, Fire and Water

Earth-based ceremonies typically begin by invoking the power and blessing of the particular locality, as well as the Directions and Elements and their associated qualities. Closure includes thanking and releasing them.

♡ Colour - used to denote particular qualities or to represent the elements and directions

♡ Smudging or 'Sweeping the Smoke' - an ancient act of purification, using the smoke from herbs to cleanse all present and create sacred space.

Readings and Inspirations

1. May you walk in beauty.
    Beauty is before you,
    Beauty is behind you,
    Above and below you.

    - Based on a Navajo blessing

2. Spirit of the East, Spirit of Air,
    of morning and Springtime
    Be with us as the sun rises in times of beginning,
    in times of planting.
    Inspire us with the fresh breath of courage
    as we go forth into new adventures.

Spirit of the South, Spirit of Fire,
of noontime and Summer.
Be with us through the heat of the day
and help us to be ever growing.
Warm us with strength and energy
for the work that awaits us.
Spirit of the West, Spirit of Water,
of evening and Autumn

Be with us as the sun sets
and help us to enjoy a rich harvest.
Flow through us with a cooling,
healing quietness and bring us peace.

Spirit of the North, Spirit of Earth,
of nighttime and winter
Be with us in the darkness
in the time of gestation.
Ground us in the wisdom of the changing seasons
as we celebrate the spiraling journey of our lives.
- Joan Goodwin, 'To the Four Directions'

3. We put our hands on the ground and ask that the great substance of the Earth give grounding to this marriage, and that the earth's beauties give it beauty. That the entire world - the animals and plants and rocks, mountains, rivers and seas, the elemental forces of earth, air, fire and water, and all the human beings - elders, children, teachers, red, yellow, black and white, be with us, teach us, show us your ways.

    And we call to the Sweet Mystery that is at the Sacred Centre to hold us and cradle us in your divine protection as you be with us, teach us and show us your ways.

We claim this marriage to serve, to bless and to share knowledge for wisdom building and for bringing wholeness and kindness to our hearts and to our world.
- *From 'Invocation Blessing Song' (adapted for marriage)*

Sikhism

♡ The Sikh word for wedding *(Anand Karaj)* translates as 'blissful event.' Marriage is a sacred bond, as two souls unite, representing the ultimate goal of merger with God.

Traditions

♡ Engagement ceremony *(Kurmai)* - the bride's male relatives visit the groom and his family with fruit and sweets. Her father fills a pink scarf on the groom's lap with seven handfuls of fruit. He then places a date in the groom's mouth, signifying acceptance of the marriage. The bride's family leave with gifts of scarves and sweets.

♡ Turmeric Cleansing Ritual *(Maiyan)* - at this joyful, messy occasion, friends cover the couple with turmeric paste to beautify the skin.

♡ Presenting Bridal Clothes and Jewellery *(Chura)* - the day before the wedding, the bride's maternal uncle gives her special clothes and red bangles that have been dipped in milk, symbolising her purity. The women continue celebrating with singing, dancing, feasting and henna painting.

♡ The bride typically wears red and sumptuous wedding jewellery. The groom, if he is Khalsa, carries a large ceremonial sword.

♡ Wedding ceremonies generally take place in the morning, at the temple.

♡ The ceremony itself:

1. The groom enters first. A special hymn announces the bride and her family. She sits or stands to the left of the groom in front of the Sikh holy book *(Siri Guru Granth Sahib)*, which is considered a sacred living presence.

2. A short blessing prayer *(ardas)* is recited, followed by a 'Guru's command' *(hukam)* from the holy book.

3. Scarf Ritual *(Palla pharana)* - the bride's father places one end of a pink or saffron scarf in the groom's right hand, passes it over his shoulder, and places the other end in his daughter's hand. The scarf links the couple throughout the ceremony.

4. Circling the Holy Book - a couple are considered married once the four marriage verses have been recited and they have circled the holy book four times. These verses were written in the sixteenth century by the fourth Sikh guru for his own wedding. They praise marriage and offer guidance for living it well. The circling and verses correspond to the four stages of spiritual development at the heart of marriage (duty to family and community, purity of mind, non-attachment, merging with divine love).

   Guests stand to support the couple as they circle, showering them with petals on the final round. The bride's family may even help her complete, as she leaves her original family to join another.

5. Feeding of Fruit - the newlyweds exchange food, committing to nourish and support each other always.

♡ Closure - traditionally the bride was carried to the groom's house in a covered litter. Today, a decorated car may drive the newlyweds to the bride's former house. She takes leave of her family there, sprinkling rice in each corner of the room as a blessing, before continuing to the groom's house for a ceremonious welcome by her new family.

Inspiration

They are not said to be husband and wife who merely sit together. Rather, they alone are called husband and wife who have one soul in two bodies.

- Guru Amar Das b.1479

PART THREE

*Post-Wedding Marriage Care
and Maintenance*

CHAPTER TWELVE

Post-Wedding Marriage Care and Maintenance

...revolutionizing the way we do our inner work and craft our intimate relationships is the most important action we can take to transform the world.
- Rob Brezsney[63]

Sometimes, in the whirlwind of preparations, the wedding day itself can seem such a monumental event that nothing exists beyond it. It can be easy to forget that a wedding heralds a whole new chapter of life.

It is the quality of the life that follows - *the marriage itself* - that matters.

I sometimes draw on this quote to remind couples: '...this wedding is only a symbol, a celebration, a public recognition of what already exists in the silent places of your hearts. It is your marriage... yours to define, yours to make real, yours to live.'[64]

---

[63] *Rob Brezsney - author, quoted on Jeff Brown's website*
[64] *Author unknown*

How do we <u>remember</u> and <u>maintain</u> the gift and deep blessing that is the essence of marriage?

Nurturing love and reverence, plus a commitment to personal growth and self-awareness are key.

The ideas, rituals and practices here are offered as guides toward creating and sustaining marital safety and vibrancy. In my view, a 'good' marriage is one that heals, spreads love and contributes to life.

Acknowledging the Spiritual Context of Marriage

A viewpoint that encompasses a bigger picture - however named - offers a radically deeper and more meaningful perspective on relationship than one which centres purely around the two individuals involved.

Essentially here, we are talking about life, with its innate intelligence, purpose and goodness, and surrendering to that. It starts with the basic premise that there is purpose in two particular individuals coming together. That life *wants* this union. Trusting life, trusting this purpose is what matters. Life wants to guide and flow through us; our task is to let ourselves be 'spirit-led.'

Honouring the Spirit of your Relationship

Marriage, like all relationships, needs tending to survive and thrive. You could consider it 'a project' coupled with friendship.

Viewing marriage as an entity in its own right can be a really helpful perspective, particularly when times are tough. The spirit of a relationship has its own needs, wisdom and aspirations. Call on it for help. An object can be used to represent it. Be open to what 'comes through' in response. Returning to memories of initial meeting, purpose and times of easy, happy loving can restore a relationship to its essential core.

Tending 'The Space Between'

Remember the importance of acknowledging the 'space between' a couple. *This is where relationships actually happen.*

Just as we cannot 'see' our relationship as a third tangible being, nor can we 'see' the space between us and our partner. And yet, we *feel* when all is well between us, and when it is not. We *know* if we are withholding or behaving in ways that distance our partner. We *sense* when love and connection flow freely and when they are blocked.

Discerning *why* there is withholding or a felt sense of distance or block can be more difficult as unconscious conditioning influences our behaviour and emotional response.

When we put love and intimacy first - above fear, self-hatred, wanting to hide, deceive or sabotage etc. - we know what is required to keep the space between us clear.

If I feel hurt by something my partner has said or done, expressing it means the emotional charge will not linger between us. 'Clearing the air' in this way means that blocks to love are not given a chance to take root.

Ideally, whilst expressing it, I can connect with what deeply matters to me beneath any judgement or blame, and perhaps connect with what might be important here for my partner too. Then I can connect with a place of tenderness for each of us and the relationship.

When we do not address issues as they arise, there is great danger that they intensify. It can take courage and vigilance to address what is obstructing that space between us. When we do, intimacy thrives.

'Handing Over' your Relationship...

This is another way of expressing the idea of honouring the spirit of a relationship or acknowledging the presence of a third 'being.'

Rather than trying to get it right all the time, how would it be to hand over our relationships to something larger than ourselves? To put ourselves in the guidance and care of life, trusting in a bigger picture.

We can be shy about talking to life, sharing our struggles, expressing our joy. Be encouraged. Take little steps. Dare to express your hopes, needs, gratitudes and fears.

Doing this keeps us alive and connected. Life can then meet and support us in our unfolding, wanting us to be whole, happy and in alignment.

Considering Soul Purpose

Marriage is a joining of worlds. It doesn't just connect two families and sets of friends; it may also bridge different cultures, faiths, or communities. It also merges ancestral lines.

Beyond this, if marriage unites two souls who have agreed to do so, this brings an added dimension to the union. Souls may come together with their own agenda, whether understood by us or not, changing our whole perspective of an intimate relationship.

Purpose and Service

When we can shift our focus from 'What can I *get?*' to 'What can I *give?*' or 'How can I best serve or contribute here?', the whole paradigm of our relationship radically alters.

Our focus can then include healing, growth, spreading joy, expressing beauty, learning reverence, praising life and experiencing union with all that is. If this becomes central to our very existence, then serving Life through our marriage is a joy, inevitably for the greater good.

Loving Personally and Impersonally

How would it be to seek the face of God in your partner or have a direct experience of seeing each other as divine beings? From this perspective, who does the washing up, sorts the finances, or mows the lawn loses its drama.

The concept of seeing beyond the personality invites loving *impersonally.* Love the unique individual before you AND, in parallel, love beyond that too.

Anything that opens our eyes to the inherent beauty, worth and goodness of ourselves and each other is a gift. By cultivating the willingness and ability to see our partner as an expression of life, our natural response is to love and praise life and creation.

Some Helpful Models, Concepts and Practices

Cultivating Gratitude

When we forget to put love first, everything suffers. One of the simplest and most powerful remedies is gratitude. An attitude of appreciation is transformative.

Let's give thanks for the life that flows through us, for the delight of our physical body, the love that we are as individuals, and the love that can be generated between us.

Focusing on the good magnifies what is already healthy and happy. Cultivating gratitude, rather than sliding into complacency or criticism, keeps us alert, present and joyful to the countless blessings that walking alongside another brings.

The Greatness of Kindness

Acts of kindness, tolerance, and generosity are the glue of relationships.

Researchers, John and Julie Gottman,[65] started observing marriages in action in the 1970s. Studies of thousands of couples led to the conclusion that 'If you want to have a stable, healthy relationship, exercise kindness early and often.'[66]

---

[65] *Drs Julie and John Gottman - world-renowned researchers and clinical psychologists, founders of The Gottman Institute*
[66] *Article 'Masters of Love' by Emily Esfahani Smith, The Atlantic June 12, 2014*

A couple bringing kindness and generosity to each other will likely thrive, whereas one dominated by criticism or hostility will not. Contempt is the major relationship annihilator. Meanness of any kind not only destroys the love in a relationship but also vastly reduces our ability to combat illness.

It was also recognised that 'people who are focused on criticizing their partners miss a whopping 50 percent of positive things their partners are doing and they see negativity when it's not there.'[67] We can be blind to the goodness and love available to us if we consistently denigrate or deny it.

Sustaining happy relationships takes effort. We can choose to grow and strengthen our 'kindness muscle.'

Finding kindness during a conflict, when it is most needed, can be the hardest thing of all. Julie Gottman emphasised this when she said 'kindness doesn't mean that we don't express our anger, but the kindness informs how we choose to express the anger. You can throw spears at your partner. Or you can explain why you're hurt and angry, and that's the kinder path.'

> *Be kind to each other, for it's really such a short journey, after all.*
> A grandmother to her grand-daughter on the eve of her wedding.[68]

---

[67] Article *'Masters of Love'* by Emily Esfahani Smith, *The Atlantic* June 12, 2014

[68] Gabriel Horn - *'The Book of Ceremonies; a Native Way of Honoring and Living the Sacred'* (2005)

Appreciate the Intention

We can easily get annoyed, irritated or triggered by our partner. Often this is because of the stories we tell ourselves or the ways we interpret words or behaviour. We can judge a situation harshly or compassionately.

For example, a woman is angered by her husband failing to put the toilet lid down. She may interpret this as deliberately uncaring when, in reality, he may have simply forgotten.

Or, picture the husband who is upset that his wife is late for the special evening out he has planned. He assumes she doesn't care enough to be punctual. She, however, had stopped to buy him a gift on the way. She arrives, happily anticipating giving her gift, only to realise that her husband is bad-tempered because he had misinterpreted the reason for her lateness.

The kind path of action lies in our willingness to respond generously to our partner's intentions. While they may have spoken or acted unskillfully, it is rare that our partner sets out to intentionally irritate, anger or hurt us. As psychologist Ty Tashiro said, 'A lot of times, a partner is trying to do the right thing even if it's executed poorly. So appreciate the intent.'[69]

In the heat of the moment, even *remembering* this point is an act of tremendous goodwill, let alone *responding* from that place. Once again, it is a practice and a choice.

---

[69] Article *'Masters of Love'* by Emily Esfahani Smith, *The Atlantic June 12, 2014*

Sharing Joy

While the importance of partners supporting each other through difficulties is recognised, research shows 'that being there for each other when things go right is actually more important for relationship quality. How someone responds to a partner's good news can have dramatic consequences for the relationship.'[70]

Researchers classified four typical responses to couples sharing good news: passive destructive, active destructive, passive constructive, and active constructive.

For example, if someone shared their excitement at getting into medical college, a passive destructive response would be to ignore the news by saying something like, 'You wouldn't believe the great news I got yesterday...!'

An active destructive response diminishes the good news by highlighting potential negatives: 'Are you sure you can handle all the studying? It takes years! And is so expensive!'

In a passive constructive response, the good news would be acknowledged but half-heartedly. For example, a distracted 'Oh, that's great, darling,' while sending a text.

Finally, in an active constructive response, the news is received wholeheartedly with something like 'That's great! Congratulations! When do you begin?!'

The first three response styles are joy-killers. The last creates an opportunity for the couple to celebrate the good news in a shared experience.

---

70 Article *'Masters of Love'* by Emily Esfahani Smith, *The Atlantic* June 12, 2014

How we respond to each other has an enormous impact. Our language and actions either disconnect or connect us.

Sacrifice

Marriage leaves us less free and independent than we might otherwise be, requiring sacrifice at times. We need to give and be available to our partner when we might not always want to.

The word 'sacrifice' conveys a sacred act, the sense of offering something precious to something precious. In the context of marriage, we offer ourselves - *we* are the gift, the most precious thing - to our partner and our relationship.

John Welwood[71] describes two very different types of sacrifice. *Neurotic sacrifice* happens 'when we try to please or placate by blindly going along with someone or bending ourselves out of shape.' It shrinks and debilitates us.

Conscious sacrifice, on the other hand, occurs when we 'knowingly choose to give up something for a greater good.' This is empowering; it helps us grow.

'Accept the Offer'

I learnt this concept from the theatre world, but it can be effectively applied to all relationships. On stage, and particularly with improvisation, actors are taught to accept the invitation that another actor offers.

This means responding to what comes your way as you each, in turn, offer and move onwards together. The

---

[71] John Welwood, *American author & psychotherapist (1943-2019) - 'Journey of the Heart: the Path of Conscious Love' (1990)*

outcome may not be known, but the dance of the journey emerges step by step.

Rejecting an offer can sometimes be helpful as it allows for alternative responses. As a general rule, however, rejecting too often tends to cause damage by eroding connection, joy and trust.

Simply put - *if your partner makes an offering towards you, accept it whenever you can.*

Research has highlighted the profound effects that accepting or declining requests have on marital well-being. Studies show[72] that divorced couples responded positively only thirty-three percent of the time, meaning that only three in ten requests for emotional connection were met. Couples who were still together responded positively almost ninety percent of the time.

Requests for connection can be conscious or unconscious, ranging from the overt to the subtle. A suggestion of a walk, meal out, or massage are clear requests for time together. Sometimes the trouble is that we do not recognise them as the signals for connection that they are.

We can be generous or less generous in our responses. If, for example, my partner enthusiastically invites me to watch football with him, my knee-jerk response would be to decline. I have no interest in football. However, when I remember that this is an invitation to join him in his world, that my presence would add to his enjoyment, this wider perspective may elicit a genuine acceptance of the offer.

Similarly, I might have spotted a garden bird and excitedly point it out. He, with little interest in wildlife, could grunt in

---

[72] *Article 'Masters of Love' by Emily Esfahani Smith, The Atlantic, June 12, 2014*

response, barely looking up. Or, *despite his limited interest*, he could respond wholeheartedly to create a completely different mutual experience.

In essence, it is not about the subject but about our willingness to generously engage with another. I am not suggesting we contort ourselves beyond recognition to please another. We must stay true to ourselves while also recognising that some responses will enhance connection while others diminish it.

A marriage is happy when the bedrock is formed of gestures that quietly affirm 'you matter to me,' 'I am interested in your world,' 'I revel in us.'

When You See, Think or Feel Something Nice About Your Partner - Tell Them!

This one is perhaps obvious and yet so easy to overlook. Make it your habit to be generous in your explicit appreciation.

If you think he looks gorgeous, or if her hair falling in just that way delights you, don't keep it to yourself - let your beloved know!

Tell her you love her, let him know how much you value his presence in your life, say the things about each other that touch, move or inspire you.

Say it out loud. Say these things as they arise, in the moment, unhindered.

When it is Easy to Love and When it is Not

The 'for better, for worse' element at the heart of some vows acknowledges the potential struggle of living alongside another. It can be hard to navigate the together-apart nature of intimacy and sustain a wholesome, beautiful marriage.

When we are in touch with the love inside us, we are open and generous. Love flows effortlessly. For most of us, this is not our constant reality. Although the *feeling* of love towards our partner may be fickle, we can remain steady in our commitment to remain *loving*, and keep nurturing our marriage, come what may.

Cultivating these loving attributes, *especially* when we do not feel them, is the challenge and the choice. Love means showing up consistently for each other and the marriage, even when difficult. It is the willingness to remember that the sun is always there, even when obscured by clouds.

Harmony, Disharmony, Repair

This concept illustrates the cycle that a healthy intimate relationship invariably moves through. Relationships are in continuous flow and, even though each stage may vary in duration or intensity, we are always in one of them.

I have come to appreciate these very different 'tones' of relationships and value how each contributes to a flourishing whole. They can help us navigate the ebbs and flows of connection, or the togetherness-apart dynamic of relationships.

We tend to shy away from the 'disharmony' element of this cycle or are conditioned to believe that a 'good' relationship is always harmonious. In addition to being untrue, it can also make it difficult to speak our truth or for our 'darker' sides to feel safe enough to offer up their gifts.

Being unmindful in the 'disharmony' stage can cause damage. It takes skill to navigate strong, intense emotions in ways that are not destructive. For example, if I can learn to listen to the wisdom or vulnerability behind my anger or irritability, I can learn from my challenging emotion without my unconscious behaviour wreaking havoc.

It is also imperative to acknowledge the necessity of the 'apart' side of the relationship dance. Western narrative consistently reinforces 'happily ever after,' idealising an unrealistic sense of uninterrupted blissful union. It negates the essential ingredient of 'pause,' where each partner regains their sense of individual self.

The potential for conflict often arises at the point in the intimacy cycle where one or the other partner needs this 'apart' time (whether psychologically and/or physically). It can be difficult to achieve the required separation. Some, for instance, only manage to reach autonomy by pushing the other away or by picking a fight. A couple may have spent a wonderful weekend together and then, pre-empting the inevitable ending and any accompanying discomfort (often unconscious), end up having a row.

Unconsciously provoking a fight can bring about the desired outcome of time apart but at a high cost. It can be horribly painful and bewildering to feel catapulted from a place of deeply bonded connection to one of strife and disconnect.

However, if these dynamics are understood as seeking to meet valid essential needs and navigated skillfully, our relationship with ourselves is replenished. Therefore, when closeness returns or is rebuilt, the re-connection is between two people who are grounded and resourced.

It can help to see conflict as an essential part of a healthy system, as supporting a return from blockage to flow. It is possible, *at any moment,* to offer a 'creative solution,' a gesture of kindness or true apology, in the midst of strife. We can either escalate conflict, or re-direct our energy towards reconciliation. We have the ability to protect or destroy one another and our relationships.

Essentially, successful long-term relationships rely not on avoiding disharmony but on both partners having the skills and willingness to repair effectively.

May we aspire to inhabit;

> the 'Harmony' stage – happily
> the 'Disharmony' stage – gracefully
> the 'Repair' stage – skillfully

> *As friendships grow closer, conflict becomes more difficult to avoid. And this is often a good thing. Because the closer we get to each other's hearts, the more triggers rise into view. Because you can't fully know someone until you ignite each other's ire. Because you won't know if a connection has legs, until it's tested by conflict. And when it is, there is a choice to be made – walk away in disgust, or walk towards in an effort to deepen the connection. Conflict isn't the adversary of connection. Fear of confrontation...is.*
> - Jeff Brown[73]

---

[73] *Jeff Brown – author and spiritual teacher*

The 'To be Right or to be Happy' Dilemma!

The simple question 'Do I want to be right or happy?' can immediately cut through to what is important. What best serves love and life - happiness or my ability to prove a point or hold my ground?

Choosing to prioritise being happy over being right aligns us, once again, with a higher principle.

Shifting from the Right/Wrong, Good/Bad Paradigm

For most of us, the concepts of right/wrong and good/bad are deeply engrained. This shaming, un-forgiving paradigm allows little room and gave us no training for compassion or understanding.

Rumi[74] - way back in the thirteenth century! - offered an alternative worldview in his poems. One of them speaks of a field 'Out beyond ideas of wrongdoing and rightdoing.' He goes on to say, 'I'll meet you there.'[75]

What if our marriages, rather than potential battlegrounds, were such a field? What if we could meet each other there, in a place beyond judgement or blame? In our own marriage, we can use this idea to transform and soften any hard edges which create distance and separation.

---

[74] *Rumi (1207-1273) - thirteenth century Persian poet, scholar and Sufi mystic*

[75] *From 'A Great Wagon' in 'The Essential Rumi,' a compilation of his poems translated by Coleman Barks*

Cultivating Attitudes of Curiosity, Fascination and Welcome

Staying in connection with curiosity, fascination and welcome automatically removes any trace of condemnation. The good/bad paradigm becomes irrelevant in the face of receptive listening and 'open' questions.

Our tendency to judge can be replaced with a willingness to remain open and to delve more deeply. Asking questions opens the way for deeper understanding.

Why', for example, 'have I just said or done that?' 'I wonder what has caused him/her to speak like that or behave in this way.' 'What is *really* wanting to be communicated here?' 'What is *actually* going on right now?

It takes time to truly listen, to hear and unravel the stories beneath the stories, the layers beneath the layers, the needs that underlie them all.

Love as a Verb

Many of us believe that love is predominantly a feeling. Feelings come and go. They tend to convey more about ourselves than anything else.

While 'love' is a noun, acknowledging it as also a verb opens up a whole other arena. *To love someone is an active experience.* It is <u>action</u> that makes love real.

> *Love is a skill, not just an enthusiasm.*[76]
> - Alain de Botton

---

76 Alain de Botton – 'The Course of Love' (2016)

Happy marriages are the result of loving choices made frequently, *whether we feel loving or not*. Yet how do we love when we do not feel loving?'

Covey gave wise counsel to a man about his ailing marriage: 'If the feeling isn't there that's a good reason to love her.... Love is a verb. Love - the feeling - is a fruit of love, the verb. So love her. Serve her. Sacrifice. Listen to her. Empathize. Appreciate. Affirm her.'[77]

'Partners' not 'Adversaries'

The word 'partner' implies equality. It speaks of mutual investment, where similarities and differences are respected and celebrated.

Many engaged couples have told me how important a sense of 'teamwork' is to them. They love that they are in something together.

Alison Armstrong[78] writes how the prevailing culture cultivates adversaries rather than partners. There is antagonism, and a power struggle between the sexes, and wounds that have been insufficiently tended. This results in hurtful behaviour, the 'little' things that, over time, erode a relationship.

We find subtle or overt ways of putting each other down. Often they pass unnoticed, having become so socially acceptable. We condone 'light' mockery of others, especially the opposite sex. We make flippant 'jokes' about how 'useless' men can be or how 'hen-pecking' women are.

---

77 *Stephen R. Covey - 'The 7 Habits of Highly Effective People: Powerful Lessons in Personal Change' (2004)*
78 *Alison A. Armstrong - Author of 'The Queen's Code' (2012)*

I am not suggesting that these behaviours do not exist – people *do* nag, folk *do* bail out on responsibilities – but meeting them with contempt never helps. In a climate of criticism, how can a loving partnership between equals of differing strengths and weaknesses ever hope to flourish?

It's become easy to 'casualise' things of great importance, even on our wedding day. At a wedding venue I temporarily worked at, there were cushions dotted about declaring 'Mr. Right' and 'Mrs. Always Right.' On one occasion, I introduced myself with 'You must be the groom?' to which the reply: 'Yes, I'm the condemned one.' Another time, I overheard a groom come straight out of the ceremony to ask the waitress to bring drinks to the guests. When she congratulated him on his marriage, he immediately quipped, 'Yep! And that's my life over now!'

Supposedly light-hearted banter, this feels beyond sad to me. It seems it is far easier to publicly joke and undermine than to champion our marriages and honour the love in our life. We seem to be ashamed to own our deepest feelings.

Please tune in to the myriad ways our words or actions bring someone down rather than build them up. Become vigilant. Refuse to lend your voice to ways that diminish another.

'The Five Love Languages'

This model comes from Gary Chapman's book,[79] which explains that people feel loved in different ways.

---

[79] *Gary Chapman - 'The Five Love Languages: How to Express Heartfelt Commitment to Your Mate'*
(1992)

Recognising our own primary 'love language' and that of our beloved can be very helpful. Understanding that there are very different styles of both expressing and experiencing love increases the chances of getting it right for our partner.

The five love languages are:

- Giving Gifts
- Physical touch
- Words of affirmation
- Acts of Service
- Quality time

These are all about giving, in one way or another. We may not always recognise them as such, particularly if our love language differs from our partner's. We tend to naturally offer another what we ourselves would love to receive.

For instance, I may often tell my man I love him or that I'm happy he's in my life because expressing words of affirmation come easily to me. This is my predominant love language and it being reciprocated helps me feel secure and loved in return.

We may come to know our own 'love language' by the ways we struggle in a relationship. One reviewer of Chapman's book described how recognising the different ways of communicating love saved her marriage. She had perceived her husband as 'selfishly wanting sex all the time' while she lamented their lack of quality time together.

Once she understood that her husband's desire for physical intimacy was an integral part of his expression of love, her outlook was transformed. For his part, when he understood how vital doing things together was for his wife, he knew what to offer.

Similarly, one person may be performing everyday tasks, happy at the love they feel they are showing their partner in such practical ways. This may go wholly unrecognised by the partner who expects household chores to be a shared 'given,' or who recognises love in the form of surprise gifts, compliments, or a hug.

'How can I be More Loving; How can I be More Kind?'

What if we made room in our relationships to ask, as fourteenth-century Hafiz suggests in his poem: 'My dear, how can I be more loving to you; how can I be more kind?'[80]

Simply ask your beloved the question, and see what happens!

One Conscious Loving Choice a Day

Commit to making one conscious loving choice a day. This simple practice prevents complacency.

> *Wake at dawn with a winged heart and give thanks for another day of loving.*[81]
> - Kahlil Gibran

Draw on your Community for Support

Marital struggle is often alleviated if we can share our grief or difficulties along the way. Our community of relatives and

---

[80] *Hafiz, Persian poet (1315-1390) - From 'It Happens All the Time in Heaven'*

[81] *Kahlil Gibran (1883-1931), Lebanese poet and philosopher - from 'The Prophet' (1923)*

friends could be a powerful resource and ally. They can offer an outside perspective when we ourselves may be too entangled to see things clearly. We need outside support to help maintain balance and strength, including in marriage.

Often we do not know how to ask for help, typically living our relationships as fairly isolated units. Our public front may differ from the life we live behind closed doors. We no longer live in small communities, where we are known and looked out for by our neighbours. Nor do we tend to live communally, where the well-being of individuals and each couple has a direct impact on the harmony of the whole.

Of course, relationships are private to the individuals within them. And yet I suggest you turn to family and friends, let your community in. Keep them, to a certain extent, included and involved in your relationship.

We have a responsibility to safeguard marriage, both our own and others.

Communication Skills

There are countless resources offering inspiring techniques and frameworks which are revolutionising the ways we behave and communicate. Old structures of hierarchy and authoritarianism are being replaced by compassion, connection, and inclusivity.

There are many ways of relating which truly honour and 'see' one another. It is not within the scope of this book to explore them in-depth, but I highlight some of the principles involved.

Learning to truly listen and hear creates connected, mature and intimate relationships. Practice with your partner, each taking uninterrupted time to share what is going on for you. The listener then reflects back what they have just heard.

Similarly, training ourselves in the arts of 'accurate empathy,' or recognising the need underlying any given utterance or behaviour, however skillfully or unskillfully expressed, sustains intimacy and brings us closer.

Marshall Rosenberg's 'NonViolent Communication' (NVC), for instance, is a language of compassion, markedly different to the one we are generally conditioned to speak. Like any foreign language, it takes time and effort to master.

Re-framing our language so that we own our feelings (rather than externalising them by attacking, blaming or projecting) is also essential.

We need to be aware that the behaviours, upsets, and patterns that we can get into with our closest ones actually ALMOST ALWAYS have NOTHING to do with the present situation. Our responses are often programmed by our unconscious mind and past experience, which means that we may well be unaware of why we react as we do.

It helps to remember that everybody is ALWAYS doing their best in any given moment. Be kind and remember that any perceived strife is an attempt to tell a story and get some fundamental needs met. *Something* is desperate to be heard, understood, and acknowledged.

The 'inner healer' in each of us re-creates scenarios in an attempt to find resolve, peace and freedom, from old wounding often buried deep within us. We 'act out' - until we don't anymore. With this perspective, our struggles are so much easier to bear.

Once we see the reason behind our 'dysfunction', purpose to our 'weaknesses,' we can recognise that our being is striving only towards wholeness, in every wise, beautiful, crazy, illogical-seeming way possible. As 'A Course in Miracles' teaches, anything that is not love is a cry for love.

Intimacy and Physical Aspects of Marriage

Intimacy should not be confused with sex. Nor with nurturing. I read somewhere that while nurturing is a form of care-taking, intimacy is a 'reciprocal expression of feeling and thought, not out of fear or dependent need, but out of a wish to know another's inner life and to be able to share one's own.'

To be intimate, then, is to be known on all levels - physical, emotional, intellectual and spiritual.

Some break up the word giving us 'in-to-me-see'. It means to see and be seen fully. It is to be 'naked' with another, whether our clothes are on or off.

Sex can certainly be a most intimate and beautiful expression of love. And it can be easy to have sex without intimacy - a sharing of bodies but not hearts - just as it is easy to have intimacy without sex. Love is the source of intimacy.

To truly love, we have to start with ourselves. To be intimate with another, we *have* to be available - connected - to ourselves first. We have to be 'at home' in order to be met or seen by someone else. We can learn to befriend ourselves, and from that truth, invite intimacy, both physically and emotionally, with another.

When we meet another from a place of self-acceptance and wholeness, we can make 'a mature choice coming from the desire to share, create, discover and celebrate existence together. Not from a place of needing someone to give you something that you don't have otherwise.'[82]

Whenever we deny our feelings, wants or needs, it is at the cost of true intimacy. It might seem 'easier' and more 'convenient' in the short term, but real connection cannot be generated when we have abandoned ourselves in the process.

Bringing awareness to our body, noticing the breath, SLOWING RIGHT DOWN and taking the time and care to be with ourselves all help us become fuller, truer versions of ourselves.

> *When you truly love yourself, when your life is full of pleasure, your cup is full. When you are full, that's when you can give. You cannot pour from an empty cup. Your cup must be overflowing, then your giving happens naturally. Someone who is nourished from within, someone who is radiant and lives in total acceptance of themselves - is a medicine to this world. Such a person gives to others simply by being. They heal the world with their presence alone.*
> - Sofia Sundari[83]

---

[82] *Sofia Sundari – mystic, author, tantra teacher www.sofiasundari.com*
[83] *Sofia Sundari – mystic, author, tantra teacher www.sofiasundari.com*

A Note on Spirituality and Sex

Some ancient teachings do not separate spirituality from what can be experienced through our own physical body.

Margot Anand, a pioneering figure of western tantra, described sex as 'both doorway to ecstatic mystical experience and an expression of the spiritual force itself.'[84] We are beginning to address the deep wounding we carry about our bodies, desires, pleasure and sexuality. Christianity established an anti-ecstatic worldview and valued pain over pleasure.

There is much to re-claim. While this may not be the path for everyone, by exploring sexuality consciously, we can heal sexual shame and trauma.

Honouring Physical and Sexual Intimacy

Although this is discussed more thoroughly in Chapter Six, I'd like to reiterate the breath-taking potential of our physical unions.

May we be generous with our touch, our presence, our attention. These are simple gifts, which can open up vastly unrealised realms of healing, pleasure, and ecstasy. Living from an awake and cherished body - each cell alive and singing - transforms life.

Each of us, doing what we can to heal from sexual wounding and shame, contributes to the collective shift in the understanding of our fundamental life force (which includes our sexual energy).

---

[84] *Margot Anand - 'The Art of Sexual Ecstasy' (1989)*

The invitation is clear: be free to appreciate, desire, adore and admire one another's physical body. Know and own your shared pleasure. This level of richness, joy and beauty is available to us all.

Our physical and sexual intimacy can be the glue binding a marriage together, infusing it with delight and fulfilment. Baba Gurinder Singh[85] advocates sex within marriage for 'brightness in the home.' Isn't that the loveliest of phrases?!

I suggest prioritising love-making, making time for it in your lives. If helpful, make scheduled 'intimacy dates' (see below) where the only agenda is to meet as authentically as possible. Bring whatever you are currently feeling (a joy, a sadness, an irritation etc.) to this meeting, working *these* as your intimacy.

'Intimacy Dates'

The invitation here is to set aside time to create intimate space together and then simply see what happens. You may like to be creatively spontaneous or take turns holding the space or suggesting a starting point.

You may want to create a certain mood or atmosphere. You may speak, write, touch, or sing, have a bath, pray, dance, make love or play. Anything is possible, as long as it is mutually wanted.

---

85   *Baba Gurinder Singh - spiritual head of Radha Soami Satsang Beas (www.rssb.org)*

Later, you might enjoy exploring some of the questions below. Devised by Jan Day,[86] they offer a guide to learning about intimacy and the ways we might block it:

Did you allow silences?
Did you let the words that were spoken touch you?
Did you get defensive?
Did you try to get somewhere?
Did your words lead to connection or disconnection, and what was your intent?
How much of yourself did you show?
How transparent were you?
What did you censor?
Did you push yourself?
Did you try to please?
Did you tolerate touch you didn't like or want?
Did you get into stories and talking about the past, or could you stay in the present?
Could you allow not-knowing?
Did you stay as an adult, or did you move into child or parent mode?
Did you want more or less touch or words? Did you communicate that?
Did you go into the unknown?
Did you catch yourself in auto-pilot?
How did you create intimacy?
How did you break intimacy?
Where was your attention - more with yourself, your partner, or between you?
Were you leading or following or a mixture of both?
Could you see the vulnerabilities in your partner in regard to closeness/separation?

---

[86]*Jan Day - UK-based relationship expert and tantra teacher (www.janday.com)*

Eye-Gazing to Promote Intimacy

Sit or lie opposite your partner and gaze softly into each other's eyes. It may just be for a few moments, to start with. The key is to stay present, remember to breathe. Stay close and true to yourself even as you allow someone else into your inner world.

Although this may not always come naturally or easily, this is a most effective way of coming into connection with another.

Knowing and Owning our Boundaries – Theory and An Exercise

I return to this essential topic because being clear in our wants, needs and desires is vital for relationships to flourish.

Conditioned to please, we may sometimes have a complex relationship with knowing what we want or need in any given moment. We are adept at over-riding our own feelings. Can you think of times when you have said 'yes' when you wanted to say 'no,' and vice versa?

Long ago, I let myself be kissed, my whole being recoiling, because I did not know how to stop the advance. My 'polite' programming ruled, and I betrayed myself, not wanting to offend or reject another.

Sometimes, we do not even know our own response. We may have lost the innate ability to hear our inner voice. Many of us have to learn to re-sensitise ourselves to even know and feel, let alone own, our yes or no.

A first step is to recognise when we go into automatic pilot. We can then practice overriding the responses and strategies we put in place long ago. This retraining of the brain can begin to create new neural pathways.

♡ An Exercise

This exercise, taught to me by Jan Day,[87] offers a simple structure in which to explore your relationship to 'Yes' and 'No' non-verbally while in connection with another. The communication expresses a wish for greater or lesser physical proximity.

'Yes' is expressed by arms at your sides, palms open and up. It communicates: 'Yes, you are welcome to come towards me.'

For 'No,' have your hands up in front of you at chest height, palms facing outwards. Feel in your body how this protects your space, signalling a 'Stop' or a pause to your partner. <u>In this moment</u>, it is not inviting closer proximity.

Face your partner at opposite sides of the room. Agreeing who goes first, one person (A) stands still while displaying either the YES or NO gesture at all times. In response to a 'Yes' gesture from A, B responds by moving forwards (= yes), or away (= no), or standing still.

Begin by closing your eyes to connect with yourself, noticing your feelings. From here, you find your Yes/No.

Throughout the exercise, the aim is to stay present, keep breathing, allow yourself to feel, and express your Yes/No. Take the necessary time for all of this to

---

[87] *Jan Day – facilitator of workshops exploring conscious sexuality and intimacy, including 'Living Tantra' (www.janday.com)*

happen... Try maintaining eye contact with your partner. This is not always easy and, in itself, is informative.

There is no touch and no talking in this exercise. The point is not how close you get to your partner but to find your Yes/No and express it *in each moment.* This means, firstly, finding your feeling and secondly, staying true to it. It also means allowing your partner to have *their* feelings.

This exercise can continue for as long as you like, though I recommend starting with just a few minutes. At an agreed signal, end this part of the exercise by returning to your own space and closing your eyes. Pause, and check in with yourself.

Mindfully, repeat the exercise while swapping the A/B positions. The third time the exercise is repeated with neither partner gesturing and *both* expressing their yes/no by either stepping forwards, backwards or standing still.

To complete, return to the original position once again, and take a few moments to connect with yourself and your experience. When ready, come together and de-brief.

This simple exercise is illuminating. It illustrates, for example, the crucial difference between us showing our partner what we would like versus a 'this is what you have to give me' style of communication.

Consciously engaging with our relationship to Yes/No can highlight our fear of giving or receiving a 'No.' We may discover that we interpret 'No' as a rejection, taking it personally rather than recognising it as information about another. We might realise that if our partner can say 'No' when they mean it, then we can fully trust their 'Yes.'

The same may be true for 'Yes.' It can be terrifying to stay true to our desire, to approach another, especially if they are expressing a 'No' in that moment.

What if we could enjoy, even *celebrate* our wanting, our desire, *regardless of any outcome*? Feeling our feelings lets us know we are alive, connected, and in touch with our life force. OUR life is living and breathing US, and this is a BEAUTIFUL THING.

This exercise allows us to simply show each other what we want. There is no hidden agenda, playing games, or second-guessing. It is not about trying to get, to please, or be 'good.'

Boundaries and Owning our Pleasure – An Exercise[88]

This exercise involves touch and giving feedback about the touch received. You can be clothed or naked, lying, standing or sitting. Establish clear boundaries before beginning. If there is anywhere you would not like to be touched, communicate this clearly (eg. I do not want my ears/genitals/knees/breasts touched).

Set a timer for however long you wish. Decide who is the 'giver,' and who is the 'receiver.' Swap roles after the allotted time. At the end, de-brief, and look after yourself and each other.

Once begun, the only words spoken are by the one receiving, and are 'Yes,' 'No,' 'Pause' and 'Please.'

---

[88] *I experienced this exercise on Jan Day's 18-month 'Living Tantra' training*

Aim to stay present and connected to yourselves and each other throughout. If the Receiver is ready to be touched, they say 'Yes.' The Giver may then touch them wherever they feel moved to (within any designated boundaries). The Receiver gives feedback *every few seconds* in the form of yes/no/pause/please.

'Yes' means something like - 'I like this. Thank you. This feels good. I am happy receiving this touch. I would love you to continue.'

'No' means something like - 'Stop. I do not like this touch right now. I do not welcome physical contact in this moment. Please remove your hand.'

'Pause' means - 'I'd like you to keep the physical connection with me, but please keep your hand still. I need a moment to take stock or to really feel what's going on for me.'

'Please' means something like - 'Oh YES! More! I am loving this; please continue! This is sooo pleasurable!'

Initially, it may feel uncomfortable to give such frequent feedback. In general, we are not used to expressing likes and dislikes in a straightforward way, so it may take practice.

It can be empowering to feel and acknowledge what you are liking/disliking in any given moment. As the Giver, it can be deeply rewarding to know that you are receiving honest feedback to the touch you are giving.

It may, at first, feel uncomfortable, even scary, to own our desires and the pleasure of physical intimacy. It can be liberating to overcome the cultural taboo which inhibits our enjoyment of touch and expression of pleasure.

'Hugging till Relaxed' – A Practice by David Schnarch[89]

This exercise involves *'holding onto' yourself while in connection with another.* It highlights some key relationship dynamics which touch on both our longings and fears of merging with another person and being fiercely independent.

Schnarch outlines four simple steps: 'Stand on your own two feet. Put your arms around your partner. Focus on *yourself.* Quiet yourself down - way down.'

Paradoxically, we have to learn to stand on our own two feet if we want to be held by another. Schnarch describes this as the key to interdependence. He maintains that 'It is only safe to focus on your partner when you have an unshakable centre within yourself.'

Ideally, each person supports themselves by standing on their own two feet, holding each other loosely. If one partner starts to lose equilibrium, it does not drastically impact the whole.

In a less ideal scenario, hugging till relaxed might involve leaning on each other. Here, the couple are using each other as support. If one wobbles, they both become de-stabilised. If one steps back, the other falls.

This exercise demonstrates that 'hugging till relaxed highlights how connection with your partner requires solid connection with *yourself*... when you're alienated from your own experience, you have no basis to feel or connect with your spouse. You have to go inward first to make a connection with yourself.'

---

[89] David Schnarch - *'Passionate Marriage: Keeping Love & Intimacy Alive in Committed Relationships'* (1997)

Whenever your loved one is furious, anxious, or stressed, the most helpful response – whether when hugging or in life - is to hold onto *yourself* and quieten down. By doing this, we look after ourselves *and* our relationship. As Schnarch says, 'the solution to marital problems' lies in 'taking better care of your own heart.'

Ritual and Sacred Space to Enhance a Marriage

Although these two themes are central to this book, I reiterate how powerful and supportive designated ritual or sacred space can be.

Let's remember that all that is required of us here is 'to show up' (whether for a moment of focussed attention, or for much longer). We do this by setting time aside, creating a conducive environment and then being available to whatever unfolds.

Spend time, alone or together, in this space. It is restorative. It helps ground and affirms the connection between a couple and, ultimately, with spirit.

Ritual has always been at the heart of indigenous cultures. Sobonfu Somé, for example, described how there were many rituals designed to support and maintain harmony and connection within intimate relationships.[90]

Some involved the individuals alone, others worked on the couple together, while yet others involved the community in providing outside support. Ritual space makes it safe to both address challenges and celebrate strengths.

---

[90] Sobonfu Somé - *'The Spirit of Intimacy: Ancient Teachings in the Ways of Relationships'* (1997)

Whether in difficulty, joy, or simple 'everydayness' with your partner, give yourselves the gift of sacred space. Unfailingly, it reminds us that we are not alone - that greater forces are available to us.

Marriage Altar

Creating a shrine to Love and to your marriage can be powerful. This is a physical space that becomes meaningful from the objects you include, the quality of time you spend here, and the intentions you bring.

In times of challenge, despair, or celebration, this special place can be visited for solace, strength, to give thanks, and ask for guidance or clarity.

Marriage Stick

This is a beautiful Native American tradition where newlyweds were presented with a marriage stick. For every happy event and every challenge faced and survived together, the couple marked a notch on their marriage stick.

Connect Regularly to your Vows

Don't let your vows be spoken only on your wedding day. Return to them often, allowing them to grow with you as you and your relationship evolve.

You could connect with your vows every day, alone or with your partner, perhaps daily for the first year, so that they become the bedrock of your marriage. Alternatively, re-visiting them each month on the date of your wedding can become a ritual of renewal, or annually returning to them each anniversary.

However frequent, each occasion is an opportunity to review and re-commit to your sacred promises.

You may find your vows need to change to reflect an even truer version of you as a couple. Re-write them, if necessary. In this way, they can continue to guide and inspire you.

Marking Anniversaries

Many couples mark their wedding anniversary as a natural celebration point of their life together.

There is the tradition of a material correlating to each year of married life, starting with paper and eventually reaching gold, emerald and diamond. This old custom demonstrates how we value marital longevity. It is considered an achievement worthy of honour and celebration.

Anniversaries are an opportunity to take stock and appreciate. How are we doing in our marriage? Are we living our vows, or would we like to inhabit them more fully? What needs relinquishing for us to thrive? Can I open my heart a little more, travel deeper into connection and intimacy with my beloved? Where is my current personal edge? What is our joint 'stretch?'

Best of all: give thanks. Express gratitude for your life and all of the love within it. Be in love - with yourself, your partner, the earth, all of creation!
Invite guidance, invoke support to dissolve *anything* that stands in the way of this.

And when the way is tough, go gently forward. Breathe and stay present, one step at a time, knowing that you are enough.

'Power Objects', including the Wedding Ring

Anything can be imbued with significance. An object becomes powerful when it has personal meaning for us. Any objects associated with your wedding or your life together can remind you of what you hold dear, and help you remain steadfast to that.

For those who exchange a ring, or other token, during their wedding ceremony, let it become a physical reminder of your vows.

Having this tangible focus can be a really helpful way of re-dedicating yourself to what matters. Simply make conscious time to connect - however briefly - with all that your wedding ring stands for.

Gabriel Horn[91] wrote of power objects typically connected with old Native marriage ways: 'By caring for such special things over time, we mirror the care that must be shown to keep a marriage strong. And something treasured, like a wedding pipe, blanket or marriage stick, becomes a physical reminder of the love and commitment that began it all. These special things can help us remember the gratitude we need to acknowledge the experience of love.'

'Sitting in Council'

This is a powerful practice within families, groups or communities. Here I am suggesting it as a tool of connection and intimacy within marriage.

One person keeps time and formally opens and closes 'council.' Within the allotted time (eg. an hour), the

[91] Gabriel Horn - *'The Book of Ceremonies: A Native Way of Honoring and Living the Sacred' (2000)*

guidelines are to 'Speak from the heart. Listen from the heart. Be sparing with our words.' This is not a place for conversation, and no-one is interrupted.

A 'talking object' lies between the couple. When either is moved to communicate, they pick up the object (in many first nations tribes, this was a 'talking stick'), and while they hold it, the time is theirs to use as they wish. Though witnessed by our partner, the communication is not aimed *at* them.

Council provides a space for each person to draw inwards and share what is alive and true in the moment. Words, movement, or silence may flow. It can be exquisite to see and get to know yourself, your partner, and your marriage from this space.

For Cleansing and Renewal

Testing times can lead to healing, growth and greater intimacy if we can **stay with** ourselves, each other, and our emotions. Rituals can powerfully address the resentments, frustrations, and disappointments which inevitably arise within relationships.

Sobonfu Somé describes traditions of the Dagara people, where couples engage in daily and every-five-day rituals of renewal. In addition, there is an annual communal ritual of atonement that particularly addresses couples. In these ways, marriage is kept fresh and alive.[92]

In the ritual that comes round every five days, a couple stand back-to-back and express any pain or frustration out loud. This is expressed to Source, to life, who can hold it

---

92 *Sobonfu Somé - 'The Spirit of Intimacy' (1997)*

all. It is not about attacking or blaming the other, nor even of being heard by our partner.

It allows a safe opportunity to release any emotional charge so that it does not become toxic. A typical pattern of escalating pain leads to some kind of cathartic 'explosion', which then subsides into release and reconciliation.

The ritual ends with the couple pouring water over each other, symbolically washing away accumulated tension. A new beginning, a clean start.

Reconnecting with Wedding Day Rituals

If your ceremony included the wine box, treasure box, or marriage candle ritual it can be really helpful to return to these, especially in times of challenge. They are a tangible reminder of the vows of love and promise made and may help restore purpose and hope.

♡ Wine Box

Open the enclosed bottle; enjoy a drink together! Talk, share, reminisce... Enjoy the love letters you wrote for one another at the time of your wedding, re-live the memories of what brought you together. Add new words if you wish to, and, of course, replenish the bottle for the next time you return to your box together.

♡ Treasure Box

As above, the treasure box can be opened on anniversaries or any other occasion - including after an argument where it can help rekindle love and promise.

♡ Marriage Candle

Light your Marriage/Unity candle whenever peace and understanding are needed. The flame can represent love and light, a reminder of vows, and of the need to bring things into the open. The light may symbolise the hope that any conflict can be quickly resolved and forgiven.

Marriage and Children

Welcoming children into the world and raising them can be one of life's most extraordinary gifts. To protect both the marriage and a thriving family life, it is vital to maintain a strong parent-to-parent bond alongside the nurture of children.

In raising a family, it can be very easy for all available energy to be channelled into the child(ren) at the expense of the adult relationship.

It is important to nurture the *foundational* relationship of your togetherness as a couple, and *from this place*, nourish and love your child.

Consciously tending the adult relationship *alongside* your parenting benefits the whole family. When the adults give each other adequate attention and support, the child has a much higher chance of receiving love and care from more fully-resourced parents.

In the stress of family life, difficulties between the parents often remain unresolved when all the focus is on the children. Ignoring issues as they come up means they can easily escalate. Neglecting the adult relationship can result in parents seeking fulfilment through their interactions with their child rather than their partner.

In summary, the same 'rules' of marriage continue to apply when children come:

♡ PLEASE love and cherish one another.
♡ Show affection.
♡ Speak your gratitude.
♡ Demonstrate your appreciation. OFTEN!

Divorce

Parting of ways, painful as this may be, is also a valid response in an intimate relationship. Contrary to popular cultural conditioning, ending a marriage does not need to equate 'failure' in a paradigm where 'success' is measured by duration rather than the happiness of the individuals involved.

Of course, I do not advocate 'throwing away' relationships simply when the going gets tough, but nor do I champion the partnerships that 'limp along,' leaving both parties undernourished and unfulfilled.

It takes discernment, honesty and great courage to acknowledge when a relationship no longer serves. Sometimes, love's greatest achievement is to LET GO for the highest good.

Chapter Summary

♥ Put love first

♥ CHOOSE to love every day; love is action

♥ Cultivate Gratitude, Kindness and Generosity

♥ Prioritise physical and sexual intimacy

♥ Celebrate Pleasure, Joy and Fun

♥ Honour and nurture the Spirit of your Marriage

♥ Be willing to see your beloved as god in masculine form and goddess in feminine form

♥ Focus on the good

♥ Love God/Life/Source through your partnership

♥ Be Devoted, Cherish and Honour one another

Gratitudes

I am powerfully indebted to all of the books, teachings and teachers mentioned throughout this book and listed in the bibliography. Whether actually quoted or not, many writers have inspired me enormously, shaped my thinking and moved me forwards in my vision and passion.

I have experienced some writings as a kind of flame in my heart, bringing me alive by awakening me to things I half knew, but revelled in them being named and articulated, to become conscious and lived. Of particular note, I am grateful to Susannah Macomb for her beautiful weaving of intercultural wedding traditions, Marianne Williamson for the spiritual framework which so overtly invites God into a marriage, and Barbara Walker for something of the woman's perspective of this rite.

Additionally, the writings of those such as John Welwood, Sobonfu Somé, Diana Richardson, Robert Fulghum and Francis Weller have struck deep chords. Their wisdom around intimacy, grief, community and ritual, and the concepts of love, grief and praise being so closely interwoven encompass what it means to me to be fully human. This grounds and anchors me; I feel held and connected by realities that weave and bind us all close. Life and love make sense to me within these frame-works. We cannot not belong. We cannot not be loved.

Special thanks to Eveline and Alex for so whole-heartedly reading the early drafts of this book and for encouraging me every inch of the way. To Gillian and Fi at the end, when I needed it. And, most of all, to my mum, Anne, for the skill and countless hours she gave as we read and re-read, shaped and crafted. Thank you so much - for giving me life, home, and unstinting love and faith in me.

For the ones that bring me ever closer to wholeness, in the knowledge of my inherent beauty and worth, I give my deepest thanks. Those friends and family who love, see and believe in me, the men I have deeply loved and journeyed with, especially the one with whom I shared heart and home while writing this book, and the one I walk towards – I treasure you all. So much.

November 2021

Inspirations and Bibliography

Chapter One

🍂 Gabriel Horn - 'The Book of Ceremonies; a Native Way of Honoring and Living the Sacred' (2005)

🍂 Gary Zukav - 'The Seat of the Soul' and 'Spiritual Partnership: the Journey to Authentic Power'

🍂 Robert Fulghum - 'From Beginning to End: The Rituals of Our Lives' (1995)

🍂 Marianne Williamson - 'Illuminata: A Return to Prayer' (1994) & 'A Return to Love' (1992)

🍂 Sobonfu Somé - 'The Spirit of Intimacy' (1997)

🍂 Martin Prechtel - 'The Smell of Rain on Dust: Grief and Praise' (2015)

🍂 Philip Zaleski and Paul Kaufman - 'Gifts of the Spirit: Living the Wisdom of the Great Religious Traditions' (1998)

🍂 Martin Shaw - 'All those Barbarians' (2020)

🍂 Brendan Taaffe, a US Singer-Songwriter

🍂 John Welwood - 'Journey of the Heart: The Path of Conscious Love' (1990)

🍂 Sofia Sundari – author and transformational leader (www. Sofiasundari.com)

Chapter Two

🍂 Robin Wall Kimmerer - 'Braiding Sweetgrass' (2013)

🍂 Zia Ali - an Interfaith Minister peer

🍂 Mac Macartney - 'The Children's Fire: Heart Song of a People' (2018)

🍂 Robert Fulghum - 'From Beginning to End: The Rituals of Our Lives' (1995)

🍂 Francis Weller - 'The Wild Edge of Sorrow: Rituals of Renewal and the Sacred Work of Grief' (2015)

❧ Robert Moore & Douglas Gillette - King, Warrior, Magician, Lover: Rediscovering the Archetypes of the Mature Masculine' (1990)

Chapter Three

❧ Barbara G. Walker - 'The Woman's Encyclopedia of Myths and Secrets' (1983)
❧ Elizabeth Gilbert - 'Committed' (2010)
❧ Mary Neasham – 'Handfasting: A Practical Guide' (2000)
❧ Esther Perel 'The State of Affairs; Rethinking Infidelity' (2017)
❧ Margaret Bennett - 'Scottish Customs: from the Cradle to the Grave' (1992)
❧ Natalie Zarrelli in a 2016 article 'For 200 Years, Secret Runaway or 'Anvil Weddings' were performed by Blacksmiths in the UK'
Website: www.atlasobscura.com/articles/for-200-years-secret-anvil-weddings-were-performed-by-blacksmiths-in-the-uk

Chapter Four

❧ Anna Franklin and Sue Phillips - 'Pagan Feasts: Seasonal Food for the Eight Festivals' (1997)
❧ Robert Lacey and Danny Danziger - 'The Year 1000' (1999)
❧ Article by Elen Sentier 'Ancient British Shamanism' in Caduceus, Issue 93
❧ Margaret Bennett - 'Scottish Customs: from the Cradle to the Grave' (1992)

Chapter Five

❧ Catherine Wright - friend and celebrant colleague
❧ Stephen Cope - 'Deep Human Connection: Why We Need It More Than Anything Else' (2019)
❧ Norman Fischer - 'Taking Our Places: The Buddhist Path to Truly Growing Up'
❧ Robert Fulghum - 'From Beginning to End: The Rituals of our Lives' (1995)

🌾 John Welwood - 'Journey of the Heart: The Path of Conscious Love' (1993)

🌾 Beloved friends Nickie Aven and Neil Giddins

🌾 Caroline Muir - 'Tantra Goddess: A Memoir of Sexual Awakening' (2011)

Chapter Six

🌾 Andrew Harvey (b.1952) - British author, scholar and teacher of mystic traditions

🌾 Barry Long, Tantric master, teacher and author - 'Making Love: Sexual Love the Divine Way' (1988)

🌾 Caroline Muir - 'Tantra Goddess: A Memoir of Sexual Awakening' (2011)

🌾 Diana Richardson, teacher, and author of 'The Heart of Tantric Sex' (2003), 'Tantric Orgasm for Women' (2004), 'Tantric Sex for Men' (2009)

🌾 Osho (1931-1990), formerly known as Rajneesh, Indian mystic and new religious movement leader

🌾 Gabriel Horn - The Book of Ceremonies: A Native Way of Honouring and Living the Sacred' (2000)

🌾 Margot Anand - author and teacher, 'the mother of modern tantra'

Chapter Seven

🌾 Mac Macartney - 'The Children's Fire: Heart Song of a People' (2018)

🌾 Sobonfu Somé - 'The Spirit of Intimacy' (1997)

🌾 Marianne Williamson (b. 1952) - American author, spiritual teacher & activist

Chapter Eight

🌾 Beverly Pagram - 'Heaven & Hearth: A Seasonal Compendium of Women's Spiritual & Domestic Lore' (1997)

🌾 Cathy Howes - 'Wedding Vows & Traditions' (2005)

🌾 Isha Mellor - 'Touch Wood: Superstitions' (1980)

❦ Anna Franklin and Sue Phillips - 'Pagan Feasts: Seasonal Food for the Eight Festivals' (1997)

❦ Brenda Knight - 'Rituals for Life' (2004)

❦ Margaret Bennett - 'Scottish Customs: from the Cradle to the Grave' (1992)

❦ Mary Neasham - 'Handfasting: A Practical Guide' (2000)

❦ Harold S. Kushner - Living a Life That Matters: Resolving the Conflict between Conscience and Success' (2001)

❦ Sobonfu Somé (d. 2017) - of the Dagara people of Burkina Faso, Somé brought her West African heritage and teachings to the West.

❦ OneSpirit Interfaith Foundation (www.interfaithfoundation.org) - Founded in London in 1996, OSIF trains interfaith ministers in the skills of spiritual counselling, celebrancy and more

❦.www.wedmagazine.co.uk/hen-parties-cornwall-devon-the-hen-revolution.html

❦ www.fizzbox.com/blog/posts/who-invented-the-hen-party

❦ www.lastnightoffreedom.co.uk/ideas/history-of-the-hen-do/

❦ www.bustle.com/articles/24357-why-do-brides-wear-veils-and-white-dresses-the-bizarre-history-of-5-wedding-traditions Article by JR Thorpe Aug 20, 2014

Chapter Nine

With special gratitude to the inspiration and sheer amount of information contained in Susannah Stefanachi-Macomb's book, 'Joining Hands and Hearts' which I have drawn on extensively for this chapter.

❦ Raven Kaldera and Tannin Schwartzstein - 'Handfasting and Wedding Rituals: Inviting Hera's Blessing' (2003)

❦ Robert Fulghum – 'From Beginning to End: The Rituals of our Lives' (1995)

❦ Susannah Stefanachi Macomb with Andrea Thompson - 'Joining Hands and Hearts: Interfaith, Intercultural Wedding Celebrations' (2003)

❦ Jane Patmore - 'Celebrate your Love: How to create a Unique, Modern and Personalised Wedding Ceremony' (2016)

❦ Rabbi Devon Lerner - 'Celebrating Interfaith Marriages: Creating your Jewish/Christian Ceremony' (1999)

❦ Mary Neasham - 'Handfasting: A Practical Guide' (2000)

❦ Margaret Bennett - 'Scottish Customs: from the Cradle to the Grave' (1992)

❦ Anna Franklin and Sue Phillips - 'Pagan Feasts: Seasonal Food for the Eight Festivals' (1997)

❦ Cathy Howes - 'Wedding Vows & Traditions' (2005)

❦ Brenda Knight - 'Rituals for Life' (2004)

❦ Allegra Taylor - 'Older than Time: A Grandmother's Search for Wisdom' (1993)

❦ Marianne Williamson - 'Illuminata' (1994)

❦ Ashley Rice - 'In my Heart' poem

❦ Neale Donald Walsch - 'Conversations with God' (a series of books published between 1995-1998)

❦ Rev Daniel L. Harris - 'Blessing of the Hands'

❦ Neil Douglas-Klotz - author and scholar in religious studies, psychology and spirituality

❦ Catherine Wright - friend and colleague

❦ Simon & Maro - dear Edinburgh-based friends

Chapter Ten

❦ Dwight B. Heath (1995) 'International Handbook on Alcohol and Culture' from https://culture.pl/en/article/a-foreigners-guide-to-polish-weddings

❦ Mary Neasham – 'Handfasting: A Practical Guide' (2000)

❦ Phillip Carr-Gomm - 'The Druid Way' (1993)

❦ Margaret Bennett - 'Scottish Customs: from the Cradle to the Grave' (1992)

❦ Jane Patmore - 'Celebrate your Love: How to create a Unique, Modern and Personalised Wedding Ceremony' (2016)

❦ Rumi (1207-1273) - thirteenth-century Persian poet, scholar and Sufi mystic

Chapter Eleven

🍃 Philip Zaleski and Paul Kaufman - 'Gifts of the Spirit: Living the Wisdom of the Great Religious Traditions' (2009)

🍃 Susannah Stefanachi Macomb with Andrea Thompson - 'Joining Hands and Hearts: Interfaith, Intercultural Wedding Celebrations' (2003)

🍃 Rabbi Devon Lerner - 'Celebrating Interfaith Marriages: Creating your Jewish/Christian Ceremony' (1999)

🍃 Matthew Fox - 'One River, Many Wells' (2000)

🍃 'Quaker faith and practice', second edition, section on 'Marriage and steadfast commitment'

🍃 Anita Diamant - 'The New Jewish Wedding' (1985)

🍃 Akasha Lonsdale - 'Do I Kneel or Do I Bow? What You Need to Know When Attending Religious Occasions' (2010)

🍃 www.interfaithfamily.com

Chapter Twelve

🍃 Sobonfu Somé - 'The Spirit of Intimacy: Ancient Teachings in the Ways of Relationship' (1997)

🍃 Gabriel Horn - 'The Book of Ceremonies: A Native Way of Honoring and Living the Sacred' (2000)

🍃 Drs Julie and John Gottman - world-renowned researchers and clinical psychologists, founders of The Gottman Institute

🍃 Emily Esfahani Smith - Article 'Masters of Love,' The Atlantic June 12, 2014

🍃 John Welwood - Journey of the Heart: The Path of Conscious Love' (1990)

🍃 Sofia Sundari - mystic, author, tantra teacher www.sofiasundari.com

🍃 Marshall Rosenberg - 'Nonviolent Communication: A Language of Compassion' (1999)

🍃 'The Essential Rumi' - translation by Coleman Barks

🍃 Alain de Botton - 'The Course of Love' (2016)

🍃 Stephen R. Covey - 'The 7 Habits of Highly Effective People: Powerful Lessons in Personal Change' (2004)

🍃 Alison A. Armstrong - 'The Queen's Code' (2012)

- Gary Chapman - 'The Five Love Languages: How to Express Heartfelt Commitment to Your Mate' (1992)
- Hafiz, Persian poet (1315-1390)
- Kahlil Gibran (1883-1931) - 'The Prophet' (1923)
- Margot Anand - 'The Art of Sexual Ecstasy' (1989)
- Baba Gurinder Singh - spiritual head of Radha Soami Satsang Beas (www.rssb.org)
- Jan Day - facilitator of workshops exploring conscious sexuality and intimacy, including 'Living Tantra' (www.janday.com)
- David Schnarch - 'Passionate Marriage: Keeping Love & Intimacy Alive in Committed Relationships' (1997)
- Gabriel Horn - 'The Book of Ceremonies: A Native Way of Honoring and Living the Sacred' (2000)
- Jack Zimmerman and Virginia Coyle - 'The Way of Council' (1996)
- 'A Course in Miracles' (1990) - no author is attributed to ACIM, although it was 'scribed' by Helen Schucman